DEAD DADS CLUB

Stories of Love, Loss, and Healing
by Daughters Who Have Lost Their Dads

Mary Burt-Godwin
www.deaddadsclub.com

ISBN-10: 0615458149
ISBN-13: 9780615458144
Library of Congress Control Number: 2011924364
Dead Dads Club Press, Carlsbad, CA

Dead Dads Club cover design by Ty Webb with inspiration from
Laura Lee Juliano-Henson and Susie Ostrowski

TABLE OF CONTENTS

INTRODUCTION

"There's a club, the Dead Dads Club, and you can't be in it until you're in it. You can try to understand, you can sympathize, but until you feel that loss . . . I'm really sorry you had to join the club."
—**Dr. Christina Yang**, *Grey's Anatomy*

I lost my father in 2001 to stomach cancer; I was twenty-nine years old, he was sixty-nine. Life as I knew it was changed forever. I began to unravel—physically, mentally, and emotionally. Thread by thread, stitch by stitch, the hole in my soul became seemingly irreparable. I couldn't get out of bed in the morning. I couldn't sleep without a sleeping pill or chardonnay. I cried, incessantly, at the drop of a hat and without warning. I felt a loneliness that could not be comforted by my family, friends, or even my loving husband. As grief took the reins, my sense of self-worth and self-esteem disintegrated. In a desperate attempt to tame my grief, I searched for solace in books and grief counseling. I wanted to hear from other women who had endured the same loss. I wanted to know I was not crazy for feeling so crazy.

Aside from a few books on the factual stages of grief, I did not find much literature detailing real-life accounts of women and what they had gone through after losing their fathers. The most powerful book I found was a collection of stories written by *Vanity Fair* contributing writer, Elissa Schappel, called *Use Me.* I related so well to her jarringly honest accounts of her father's battle with cancer, her rebellious backlash, and her grief after his passing. Though her words brought out the ugly cry, they helped me begin to heal, and made me feel like I was not so crazy.

A few months later, while watching an episode of *The Oprah Winfrey Show*, I saw an emotional Gwyneth Paltrow open up to Oprah about the death of her father. I was glued to the TV. Words like *debilitating* and *derailing* fell from her lips as she fought back tears. I could feel her pain through the screen. She was describing my life. This seemingly perfect celebrity had experienced the same pain that I had been feeling, and somehow that gave me solace.

That night, I wrote this in my journal:

Publish a book about strong women who have lost their dads: they tell their stories to help their own grief process and also to help others who are experiencing a similar loss.

With that sentence, this book was born. I didn't act on it for another few years until I was a stay-at-home mom, desperate for a non-Disney-related project of my own. Between nursing and changing diapers, I opened up my contact list and began calling or emailing every woman I knew who had lost her father—friends, family, former co-workers, everyone. Their overwhelmingly positive responses were all I needed to know that I was on the right track.

My next step was to use the Internet as a portal to reach

women from all walks of life. I began a blog and posted my request for submissions on websites dedicated to women's issues. I soon had hundreds of women interested in the project. Not all of them felt up to the challenge of writing, of tapping into those feelings, but all of them expressed their gratitude for the project and encouraged me to complete my mission.

I received a wide variety of submissions from narratives to poems, memoirs to eulogies. Each time I read a story, I was touched that regardless of the woman's experience with grief or how her father had passed, I could relate to some aspect of it, even if it was only one line or thought. There was always at least one nugget of truth for me to relate to. Each story unique, but the pain, universal.

I found it interesting to read about the various coping mechanisms that the contributors adopted. Some found God, some found the bottle, and others found productive avenues to honor their dads. It became clear that there is no playbook for grief; we all just do the best we can to get through. For me, writing about my dad and creating this book have been the crux of my coping.

This book is an ode to my dad. It's a therapeutic glass of wine with the women of "the club" who want to commiserate and celebrate their losses together. My hope is that this book brings healing, hope, and light through the fog of grief and may even inspire you to write a story of your own.

I now call to order the first meeting of the Dead Dads Club.

Mary Burt-Godwin

CHAPTER ONE:

LIFE WITH DAD

Life with my dad had its ups and downs. Like many father-daughter relationships, it was often a justice scale tipping between love and hate—but mostly it was love.

As a little girl, I would sit on his shoulders, feeling like my head was going to touch the clouds. I was happy, full of song, and safe, yet a few moments later, I would be atop the staircase, listening to the unkind words exchanged between him and my mother; my source of protection from hurt, was, at times, the cause of it. Life continued like that, up and down, through adolescence and into adulthood. At some point in my twenties, things changed. He retired from practicing law, laid off the sauce, and began to smell the roses, and I began to appreciate his Republican diatribes and overbearing ways rather than dread them. We could talk as adults, and I sought out his advice. By the end of his life, we had shared a multitude of wonderful times together—we were closer than ever, and then he was taken away.

The following pieces give us a glimpse into various father-daughter relationships. They show us that each woman's relationship with her dad is different than any other. Some are close, some estranged, some a combination of both. Regardless, we miss our dads once they are gone. We will always be that little girl sitting on our daddy's shoulders.

Tap 'Er Light

Whirling, swirling, torrential rainstorm and thunder balls, intense lightning, black night, and I could hold your hand tightly and fear no longer. During a storm, Mother used to call out your name, "Sam, do something," because she knew of your superhuman powers to quell the Midwest storms.

Tears, stress, angst, emotional tumult, and you held my hand tightly until my upset had passed.

You held my hand, and the world was safe.

You held my hand, and your energy protected my soul.

I keep your name close to my heart and share your stories with my children and granddaughter. You were a funny man who could have been a successful, beloved professor instead of a successful, beloved entrepreneur. Your storytelling is legendary to this day, especially your fishing tales.

You worked hard and long to provide me with everything, everything you could imagine would please me. You gave graciously as well as generously. I learned to love your surprises: a trip to the toy store, a bike, a scooter, water skiing, sneaking off on a school night for a jaunt to kiddy land. Glee arises within me at the mere memory of so many fun times. Glee is the word that captured each moment, and glee was your goal, always achieved.

You respected and adored our mother. Home for lunch just to see her and share a laugh. Home for lunch just to catch her in the yard, standing on her head in a yoga pose. Home for lunch to steal extra moments of family enjoyment.

I remember you singing silly bird songs at my bedroom door to awaken me early. You did not want to eat breakfast alone, and since Mother refused to rise, I was sought as your dining partner. No matter how I resisted, your cajoling won me over and got me out of my warm, cozy bed. We talked and ate, and you were interested in hearing about my teenage life. Joyfully you left for work as if my words and wisdom had enlightened and brightened your day.

Dad, you showed me that life is good by your words and deeds, but you did not prepare me for your absence. I believed we would go on forever.

Then you went away, just dropped out without a sound or a goodbye. I had to learn new ways of thinking. Without warning and without a word, Mother expected me to take care of business in your absence. I let go of your hand and faced the whirling, turbulent rainstorms on my own.

The gravestone stated the usual information plus the line, "Tap 'er light," a phrase you learned while working on your master's degree in metallurgical engineering. You oversaw copper mines in Cuba and diamond mines in South Africa. The miners were reminded daily of the fragility of their surroundings and, for their own survival, were reminded to "tap 'er light." Strike too hard on the fragile walls of the mine, and your world could cave in on you. You often quoted "tap 'er light" to remind us to work but work with forethought, purpose, and structure. After many decades, brother Howie and I still struggle with finding the balance.

Your goodness lives on in me, and I strive to share goodness with my family and the world. I strive to honor you and your lessons. Often, I ask myself how you would handle the storm imminently approaching me and wish I could hold your hand again to turn away the thunder.

Tap 'er light, Popsie.

Norma Hirsh

Don't Get Sick, or Your Father Will Die

Don't get sick, or your father will die.

My mom sent me off to grammar school every day with these words. I took the responsibility seriously, doing my darndest not to catch any of the bugs hiding in the ancient school walls.

The first forty-nine years of my life were dominated by the impending death of my father. Ten years before my birth, my dad had been given six months to live; that would have been in 1939. He passed away in 1999, having outlived some seventeen doctors and virtually every one of his male friends.

So my story is a little different from the stories of others. Yes, I was surprised when he died at the age of eighty-eight, surprised because he never died any of the other times when it had been a sure thing. I was also surprised that he'd been alive to see me graduate from high school, then college, to see me marry (three times), and to know and love his granddaughter and to see her graduate from high school.

As a teenager, my dad served in the U.S. Navy, working in the boiler room of early submarines; when the boiler steamed over, my dad's lungs got fried. By the time he was nineteen, he had the use of only one-third of one lung, hence the prediction of death at a young age. Because he was very vulnerable to any pulmonary infection, my brother and I were instructed not to bring home any colds.

What was confusing to me as a young girl was how to reconcile the image of my dying father with the man who worked fifty or more hours a week in a factory, coming home precisely at 5:15 p.m. and expecting dinner on the table at 5:30. British-born, my dad was a stoic who never once complained about feeling ill or having difficulty breathing, and so it was hard to see him as frail just below the surface.

When I was twenty, my parents arrived about two hours late to the rehearsal dinner for my first wedding. I was embarrassed by their rudeness. The next day, my father walked me down the aisle. Only after returning from my honeymoon did I learn that he'd been hospitalized immediately after I left the wedding reception, remaining in the intensive care unit for more than a month. He was an expert at not showing pain. Ten or fifteen similar episodes dotted my life.

I learned as a little girl always to be prepared for a funeral—specifically, my father's. Over the forty-nine years that my dad and I shared on the planet, I probably owned seven funeral dresses. I had mini-dresses, dirndl dresses, empire dresses, long dresses, and, I'm embarrassed to admit, a baby-doll funeral dress. I learned to always be ready, to have the right black shoes and pearls waiting to be packed. Sometimes the emergency calls came during the day, sometimes at two in the morning. Sometimes I lived only a small New England state away, sometimes three thousand miles across the country. It didn't matter. I was always prepared.

I drove during the day or flew during the night, made arrangements at school, made arrangements at work, had contingency plans for childcare and pet care. On arrival at a hospital, the drill was always the same: I would locate his room, meet with my mother and brother, speak to various doctors, and learn that my dad had, perhaps, hours to live. We would gather around his bed, holding hands, saying goodbye, and tearfully acknowledging how lucky we'd been to have him around this long. Then he would recover. Sometimes the turnaround was gradual, and other times it came with extraordinary rapidity. On one occasion when he was unconscious, he suddenly opened his eyes and told a joke. Once the word spread around the floor, a parade of hospital staff trooped in to see if he really had revived.

Even when my dad was transferred to the hospice unit at the Phoenix Veterans Administration hospital, I didn't think he was really dying. Even when he called at eleven at night, barely able to speak, to say goodbye to me and tell me that he loved me, I didn't think he would really go. When my brother called four hours later to tell me he'd passed on, I didn't believe it. All those years of blessed false alarms, all those experiences of unnecessary yet painful grieving, had resulted in some serious magical thinking on my part.

He was, in fact, dead this time. He had lived all of his lives, and there would be no more happy surprises. All of my years of preparing for his death did not prepare me for the reality of it. As I spoke to the crowd gathered at his memorial service, a part of me still thought it might be a dream, that he might stand up from a pew and say something funny, but the wiser part of me knew he was gone. His stubborn will to live could no longer give me a reprise.

My dad was, above all, a good and honest man, a steady provider for his family, a man who would not give up on life. I am glad to be my father's daughter and to be Jo Wayles, as he was Joe Wayles.

Jo Wayles

Bury Me in My Sneakers

My father, Chuck McCartney, died on June 2, 2005, my parents' fifty-fourth wedding anniversary, when he was eighty years old. Six days later I turned forty-four. My cousin Meg took us all to the New York Athletic Club to celebrate my birthday, and the background music was all my dad's favorites—Glenn Miller, Frank Sinatra, the oldies but goodies. I had my face in my hands during the whole meal, crying. My cousin tipped the manager to put on anything but sentimental music.

Although my father was fighting brain cancer and had beaten lung cancer four times, he ultimately died of pneumonia. We were not ready for Dad to go, but he was. We had scheduled hospice for him the next day, but I guess he heard it was happy hour in heaven or something, because he checked out that night.

When I knew the end was near, I quit my job in Chicago and moved back to New York to be with my parents. I was the youngest, single, had no kids to worry about, and had been looking to make a change with my job anyway. I accepted a position with a different company, a competitor with my former employer, and have been much happier; things do happen for a reason

I thought Dad had about six months left, but he died within two days, and it was brutal. My grieving process took on a life of its own. Those first few months, my mom, my sister, Mary, and I drank a lot of wine every night. It dulled the pain a bit. We talked about him, remembering all the funny things he said and did. Dad was quite a character and often confused words and terms. If he had a premonition, he would call it ESPN; when giving a speech at the Waldorf to his associates at Union Carbide, he said, "Our company is branching out like the testicles of an octopus." He brought the house down.

I worked from my mom's house in Pelham, New York, for the entire year after his death. It was a tough year, but being with her felt right, and I know being together helped us both. My sister lived in New York City and was always the one to be there for everything, so it seemed like my chance to pitch in. We were like The Three Musketeers; we took lots of trips and had great dinners with friends. I will treasure those memories forever. Sometimes, though, I felt like I was going through the motions of living; nothing seemed normal anymore without my dad.

I dream of the day when we will all be reunited with my father in heaven. If someone told me I had a week to live, I would be sad to leave everyone on this earth, but I would be so excited to be with my dad that I would have them bury me with my sneakers so that I could run into his arms again. I know that heaven is a much better place because he is there, and I bet he has already met all the fun people to whom he will introduce me the moment I arrive.

At his funeral, my mom read my nephew Charlie's beautiful tribute to my dad, which was a part of his application to Princeton University. Ironically, he graduated from there on June 2, the date of my parents' wedding and my dad's death.

Then I gave the eulogy. I was not sure I would be able to get through it, but I did, knowing that it was my last chance to make my dad proud. I opened it with the words given to the Tin Man in *The Wizard of Oz*, "A heart is not judged by how much you love but by how much you are loved by others." Everyone loved our dad. He was the kindest, sweetest, gentlest man we'll ever know.

Margie McCartney

Run Daddy, Run

My father, Joseph Albert Rueff, was a rough-and-tumble fellow. His gruff voice and beard gave him a "Grizzly Adams" sort of appearance. In addition, he wore a camouflage military jacket, his favorite cap with the fishing hook attached, and fingerless gloves that helped him more easily maneuver his wheelchair. As a double amputee in this get-up, he appeared to be a war veteran, and I suppose he was, although he had never been in the military. He attended Kentucky Military Institute, which is where he gained his military presence, and he fought a battle with Raynaud's disease that ultimately took both his legs and several fingers.

He lost his first leg when I was eight and the second when I was sixteen. He had high blood pressure, kidney failure, high cholesterol, poor circulation, and ultimately died from congestive heart failure. There was rarely a day he felt great, but he didn't let that show. His battle with health issues was long and arduous, but the things I remember most overshadow the hospital stays and the constant, terrifying beeping of machines with tubes running in every direction.

I remember that my father was a jovial man with a hearty laugh. He loved fishing, and we went often. I have a treasure trove of memories from our fishing expeditions on Kentucky Lake. It wasn't until years later that I realized these trips weren't just for the fish. We talked about everything from the mundane to our dreams of the future. I remember passing signs for the latest lottery jackpot and spending that money for the next thirty miles. He was full of life, and what my brothers and I now call "Rueffisms"—pearls of wisdom that at first seem utterly nonsensical but upon further examination project wisdom and his innermost hopes for his three children. My brothers and I were told, "If it's worth doing, it's worth doing right the first time," a life lesson that we heard over and over because we tried to cut corners and almost never got away with it. I loved our talks at the lake and the way we jammed to James Taylor and ZZ Top, winding along country roads on the way back home. He was the smartest man I've ever known.

Even after I married and moved away, I called Daddy nearly every day. I called him the morning of the day he died, and I will always be grateful for that. He was upbeat, having the time of his life, and putting new weights on his lines for an upcoming fishing trip. He told me that he was feeling better than he had in a long time. We talked about the beautiful spring weather, the new house that my husband had just built, and how he was looking forward to our visit with the kids. He died at 10:40 that night, so we saw him sooner than we had expected. He was calm and smiling, among mountains of roses and lilies, his favorite flowers.

I know Daddy is fishing in heaven, and now that he has his legs back, he's probably pulling a Forrest Gump and running all the time. He's been gone almost three years, and I still talk to him daily. I miss hearing his voice.

Amy Lepore

Wherever You Go, I Shall Follow

A child of the Great Depression, my dad was a quiet, stoic, ethical giant of a man. Standing six foot five, he was a gangly Eagle Scout who went to community college and then to Antioch College in Yellow Springs, Ohio, graduating from its work-study degree program. He met my mother there, and she quit school to marry the older man she adored. My mother's parents both died before she turned eleven, so when she met Dad, he was the knight in shining armor she'd always dreamed of, carrying her away to the exotic land of Long Island, New York. He worked as an electrical engineer at a defense company for more than forty years.

Dad was patient, frugal, detail oriented, intensely loyal, self-reliant, and fair. He was a strict conservative and could rail loudly about the evils of liberalism and Communism. He enlisted in the Navy, but World War II ended while he was in boot camp. He believed that serving in the military was one of the most important duties of an American.

Dad was also incredibly handy and loved to work around the house or yard. His basement workshop was a world of wonders to me: jigsaw, table saw, vises, wood glue, racks of screwdrivers, pliers, hammers, and odd-shaped tools from his beloved Sears® catalog. I easily recall the smell of fresh-cut two by fours and the piles of golden sawdust that covered his Hush Puppies® as he bent over his workbench.

Outside, I was equally fascinated with the sound of his gear: the riding lawnmower, the chainsaw, the weed whacker, and even the generator. He built a shed, which housed this paraphernalia, along with our three-speed bikes and tetherball equipment. The day I was old enough to mow the lawn was momentous, and I remember climbing onto the lawn mower as if I owned the world.

I took for granted the world he created for my mother, my three sisters, and me. We lived on nearly three acres of heavily wooded land. He laid the railroad ties that lined our driveway, planted the annual Christmas tree, painted the trim, and created a vegetable garden. He hung the badminton net, poured concrete for our swing set, and built an outdoor shower so that we could rinse off after a day at the beach. He crafted the built-in desk and bookshelves for the room I shared with my sister. He removed the kitchen cabinets that blocked the view from the kitchen to the breakfast nook "because your mom asked me to."

We would compliment his work and say "that's nice" to him, but as kids, I'm not sure we ever really thanked him. He just felt good doing it and loved to keep busy. I'm sure my mom thanked him in her own way. They never improved their own bedroom, and I learned later in life that that is what parents do—they spend their time, energy, and effort making life better for their children. "I don't need a new bureau," he'd say.

The early phase of my life, through high school, was its own chapter in my relationship with my father. I often felt that I was the son in the family of four girls. I tended to spend the most time with him in the basement workshop, volunteered first to go fishing with him in our little motorboat, accepted the occasional offer to play chess, and bundled up to help him cut wood from the downed trees in our backyard every fall. We never talked a lot. Dad seemed to get his peace from having someone near. My own son has the same tendency. He doesn't say a lot, but he notices the moment I rise to leave. He glances up and says, "You leaving?" I hear my dad's voice when my son asks me that.

My mother was diagnosed with cancer in 1974, at the age of forty-four, and six years later, she died. I was twenty-one and in my final year of college; this began the second phase of my relationship with Dad. We had been a very mother-dominated family until that point; she stayed at home, volunteered at school and for carpools, made dinners, helped with homework, and built a life for herself with my father. Life was about to change.

I remember feeling surprised the day after Thanksgiving when Dad told us we were going to scatter Mom's ashes in Long Island Sound. He drove us to the beach and handed out the carefully copied scripture readings and poems for each of us to read as we stood on the large boulders uncovered by low tide. Water was all around us, and the sun was meager in the winter sky. He read a scripture from the book of Ruth that includes the line, "wherever you go, I shall follow," and I saw the incredible pain of loss wash over his face. This was the face of pure sorrow, the type of sorrow you have when you've lost your one true love. I felt like I was seeing my father as a man of deep emotion, conviction, and love for the first time.

The next day, I was in our back yard raking leaves with Dad. It was mid-afternoon, still cold and cloudy, but I knew that Dad needed help with the piles to be raked, and it was my turn to help. As usual, he was very quiet, and our con-versational style was caring but brief. "You start there" and "Need some gloves?" and "Getting colder—do you need a warmer jacket?"

Suddenly Dad leaned on his rake and paused. I sensed something was up. He looked at me and quietly asked, "Did she ever talk about me?"

We stood leaning on our rakes and talked about Mom for hours—her life, her passing, her meaning, her contributions, and her obvious love for him. He poured out questions and comments in an unprecedented flow of words and thoughts. I wish I could remember more about that conversation, especially the details. However, the feeling of that afternoon is as real and fresh as if it were yesterday. Dad spoke to me as an adult, as a woman, as a child, as a comforter, as a memory book, and as a sounding board. I consider it a watershed day in my life with him, and my perception of him as a complicated man of love, loss, passion, anger, fault, and devotion was cemented in my mind.

The next twenty-five years represent the final phase of my relationship with my dad; it was one that I appreciated increasingly as time passed. He remarried in 1986 to the woman down the street, JR. She was a widow who loved to travel and had an enormous sense of adventure. Their lives were happy and full of tremendous experiences abroad; it was nice to see Dad so active and happy, and his new wife was so unlike my mother that it was easy to accept and like her.

I moved on with my life—attended graduate school, got married, and had children of my own. During weekly phone calls, I'd update Dad about my life, and he eased back into his sparsely worded conversational style: "That's nice" and "How're the kids?" I was very happy with this, as I knew he drew strength and comfort from hearing from his children and learning of their lives.

Other moments stand out. When my son was diagnosed with epilepsy, I remember calling my dad in tears. At age forty-two, I still needed to hear his voice of comfort and reassurance, reminding me that all you need to do is love a child and all will be well.

The end of Dad's life began with the death of JR; it is still agonizing to recall this painful period. She died on Earth Day, April 22, 2008. It was a fitting day, as she was a champion gardener and had a loyal apprentice in my father. He made his springtime trips to the garden store, planted small trees, trimmed shrubs, and learned how to plant more than 200 tulip bulbs. She had been sick for months, and he made twice-daily round trips to the hospital or nursing home, ten to thirty miles away. Loyalty, devotion, and support were built into his character. "In sickness and in health," he'd tell me.

It seems that perhaps Dad's devotion to his wife caused him to ignore his own worsening health. While he did his best to care for himself, he postponed much-needed care. In early June, he was diagnosed with heart failure, requiring a valve replacement. I had just been to New York in April when my stepmother died, but something told me that I had to be there for his surgery in June.

Dad's surgery went well, but sadly, his recovery was excruciating. I flew from California to be with him for nineteen days, giving some respite to my three sisters who'd rarely left his side since his wife died. I spent eighteen nine-hour days by my dad's bed in intensive care, where he was on life support and never awoke. On my last day there, he opened his eyes and was able to communicate with me.

Dad slowly improved but remained on a ventilator, with unstable blood pressure and numerous infections. After six weeks, Dad was moved to Johns Hopkins Hospital in Baltimore, to be closer to my sisters. We realized that his recovery was going to be very slow, but perhaps the tide was turning in his favor.

I came to visit him again in early August and was able to spend some wonderful time with him. He remained on a ventilator, unable to speak, but we quickly established a communication system. During my visit, the Summer

Olympics opened, and every TV in the twenty-eight-bed ICU was tuned to the games. It seemed that the feelings of hope, inspiration, and determination the stories conveyed were contagious to the patients. Dad watched it for hours. During this time, I witnessed him standing for the first time in eight weeks. I cried with joy. He told me he wanted to sit in a chair; I replied that it was so he could get closer to the TV and watch his favorite event, women's beach volleyball. He laughed. At this time, it seemed possible that, though the road would be long, he might make it. Sadly, I was mistaken.

Dad died on Tuesday, September 2.

My three sisters were by his side when he passed, but I was with my family in California. I remember the intensity of the physical sensations, pulling me into raw, opposing emotions, agonizing grief, and utter relief. Dad was gone but his pain was over.

The changes in me since Dad passed are substantial and everlasting. While many are subtle, the most significant change simply has to do with my outlook on life. Always an optimist, I've become even more committed to living life and not waiting for the perfect opportunity, possession, relationship, or experience. My time with my children, my relationships with my friends, and my commitment to my marriage, my family, my health, and my personal life are renewed and newly enhanced.

I loved my father and believe that he ran into my mother's arms when he died. I get immense peace from this image and am comforted that he is with our Father forevermore.

Julie Ames

From Guilt to Healing

Almost three years after losing my father, I am conflicted. For years I thought I wouldn't be able to survive without him, but at times, I now feel, with a stab of guilt, that my life is almost better since he's gone.

Our relationship was not stormy—we rarely fought, but there were black clouds hovering overhead. I lived at home, sharing the railroad apartment I grew up in with Dad. In a way, it was a good arrangement. The rent was cheap, and my dad and I could keep each other company. When my two sisters and I were teenagers, my mother left. As kids, my father used to joke that if Mom came home a little late from work, she was running away with a sailor. It turned out that she picked a co-worker instead. Though we all survived, it was devastating for my recently unemployed father, who already suffered from depression and alcoholism. Between that and the back injury a few years later that kept him from working his warehouse job, the last decade of his life was spent mostly at home. He lived off a veteran's pension and what we daughters chipped in, which was meager during our college years. My sisters married young, after which I found myself in an almost roommate-type situation with Dad. This worked well for both of us. We could talk for hours, or sometimes I'd just keep him company while he watched TV. Dad was highly intelligent and one of the funniest people I've ever known.

There was a dark side to our life together. His depression made him withdrawn, and even though he drank sporadically in his last years, his dependency on pain medication and his lack of interest in life took its toll on me. I worried constantly about losing him. He would tell me that he stayed alive only because he loved his daughters, then he would try to assure me that I'd do fine, probably better, once he was gone. Anytime he'd bring that up I would get highly agitated, usually retreating to my bedroom and feeling ill. Few things in life worked me up that much.

The facts worried me. Dad always emphasized that many alcoholics don't live past the age of fifty, and as he reached the latter part of that decade, there were signs that he was right. The pain meds and his lack of activity, besides the occasional long walk, impacted his health badly, particularly his heart. Knowing this led to my habit of checking the apartment when I came home if he wasn't there to greet me, thinking I'd find him unconscious or worse.

Finally, in July of 2006, my fear was realized. On a stifling hot day during a week-long blackout in Queens, I came home from work to find my father on the kitchen floor. I knew he'd been drinking, and I always stayed with my sister during those episodes, but I'd come home after a few days when he'd pulled himself together. On this day, though, I'd come to check up on him and see if I could talk with him about the situation, but when I saw him lying there, I immediately ran over to try to wake him up. He'd passed out before, and usually I had only to yell really loud to get him to stir. When that didn't work, I checked his pulse and realized how cold he was. When the ambulance came, the medics confirmed what I was trying not to conclude: he was already gone. I went into autopilot while I got in touch with my sisters, spoke to the emergency workers, the police, and the medical examiner. I had to explain in a haze who I was and what had happened to my father. Curious people from the block, lacking TV and air conditioning due to the blackout, got the full spectacle of three overwhelmed daughters and two husbands trying to keep it together.

The months following his death were hellish. Between coming to terms with losing Dad and cleaning up three decades of clutter in the apartment, I slept very little for the rest of the year. I put on weight, and my twenties caught up with me. I went from "you look like a teenager" to "so, you're turning thirty, huh?" When I did sleep, my dreams were troubling. At times I dreamt that he wasn't really dead, he'd just gone away for a while. Sometimes he'd die all over, in front of me this time, and it could be graphic. I thought about getting medication for anxiety, but I didn't want to become dependent on medication. I did occasionally make myself a drink before bed, something I almost never did in front of my father, because I thought it'd be cruel. Of course, drinking only helped me fall asleep; I'd wake up in the middle of the night, worried about my finances or terrified of the roaches that had surfaced during the summer. I'd always had my dad to take care of that. I felt lonely and horrible that my father had died alone.

Still, there were a lot of positive moments, when my friends and family all came together to make sure that I was okay. Of course, my sisters were grieving, and though they had great support from their husbands, it was a relief that we all lived nearby and could talk about our pain with each other. My decorator friend got a bunch of people to help renovate the apartment, which I decided to stay in. One of my closest friends and her husband even took care of making the kitchen look entirely different. It was their last mission in New York before moving permanently to Florida. My friends understood how important it was that my home looked different so that the memories wouldn't haunt me as much.

Though I was completely grateful for everyone's help, I was in terrible inner turmoil. When I stopped being angry at my father for leaving me alone, I began the full process of truly missing him. Though we were always pretty open with each other, there was so much more I'd wanted to say to him: how much I loved him and just how thankful I was he'd stuck around after Mom took off. I regretted that I'd had him for only twenty-nine years. I used to sympathize with him for losing his own father when he was twenty-nine, but his father was eighty-three when he died, so it made a little more sense. Dad lived to only fifty-eight.

What bothered me the most was the guilt, for I began to see that in many ways, my life improved after he was gone. I began to keep my home in good condition and became more organized. Now I'm able to have friends over, as well as over-night guests, the way I never had a chance to do growing up. For the most part, I've lived on my own the past two years and have found that I'm a capable woman after all. I've also come to appreciate my extended family more since I don't have Dad as a go-between, though I still don't call them as often as I should. I'm acting like an adult, at least usually. Dad was right. I am better off, and though that is good for me, I feel terrible about it sometimes. I know that he would never have wanted me to feel bad about the improvements in my life, and if he could see me now, he would be more than happy that I am all right.

Though through my faith I know I'll see him again, there are still days I wish I could sit and talk with him over tea, like we used to, with the TV on in the background or on one of our walks to the park. I want to tell him about what's been going on in the world, what's happening on *House*, who's had babies, or the funny things the cats did yesterday. Watching the 2008 election coverage would have been much more interesting with his commentaries, I'm sure.

I'm thankful for the time I did have with him and am glad he's no longer in pain. Now I live with him only through memories, photographs, and the few things of his I kept. Most precious to me, though, is sharing Dad with those he loved and who love him now. We can actually laugh sometimes about the time spent with him, the stories he told, his odd nicknames for people and pets alike, and his affectionate nature. In this way, I am healing, and life goes on, just as he would have wanted.

Catherine Thom

His, Hers, and Ours

In February 2001, I sat in a doctor's office, hearing an oncologist say that my stepdad had only months to live. I felt a surprising sense of sadness, surprising because I had not been extremely close to him, and an overwhelming sense of fear, overwhelming because there was so much unknown—how long did he have, would he be in pain, and how would it feel to lose him? Though he was not my real dad, my feelings were real, as real as that tumor in his liver.

My relationship with my stepdad began when I was fourteen, after he and my mom reconnected at their twenty-year high school reunion. My mom had been raising my brother and me by herself for several years after she and my birth father divorced. Moving from Scottsdale, Arizona to San Diego, where my stepdad was a practicing attorney, in the middle of my high school years was a rough adjustment for me, but I survived. I was full of resentment because I had to leave the city that I grew up in and had to leave all my friends I had known for so many years. I had no idea what to expect living in a new city, far away from my real dad and living with a man I barely knew.

My stepdad took us in as part of the family and was, overall, very generous and supportive. The dynamics of being a stepdaughter to a man who has three daughters of his own from a previous marriage are complicated. There seemed to be a constant battle between my mom and stepdad over her kids and his kids. This led to some heated arguments and much tension on the home front. A few years later, my mom became pregnant with a child of their own, so then we were dealing with "his, hers, *and* ours."

This seemed to calm things down a bit as they now had a child that belonged to both of them. Their love for this baby girl was healing for the relationship. I saw a loving and gentle side to him as he interacted with my new half-sister. It was consistent and unconditional love, something I had not seen from him before.

As time passed, my stepdad continued to provide for me and be as much of a father figure as he was capable of. When I got my driver's license, he let me drive his pride and joy, an orange '69 Camaro. Shortly after that, he helped me buy my first car. In his own way, he was showing me that he truly did care.

Through the years, my respect for my stepdad grew, and although there was never a strong bond between us, I knew that he was there for me in any situation. When I was engaged to be married, I had a huge dilemma. I wanted my real dad to walk me down the aisle, but he was not in a position to pay any of the expenses of my wedding. I knew that my stepdad would graciously pay, but I was worried he might be offended if not asked to give me away. He and I had an open and honest discussion about it. He turned out to be very understanding and was okay with my desire to have my own father give me away. After that talk, I became even closer to him, as he showed me compassion in a way I had never before felt from him before.

I truly grew to love him and hoped that he loved me, but I knew it was not the same kind of love that he had for his own daughters. I was able to accept that.

During the last few days of my stepdad's life, I was able to open myself up to him in ways I never had before. I told him, "Thank you for taking me in as a stepdaughter and sharing your love and your life with me." I am so glad that I was able to communicate that to him before he died.

I will always have love, respect, and gratitude for my gentle-giant stepdad who did his best to be a father to me.

Laurie Houston

The Benevolent Dictator

In the first few days after my dad died, I could not believe there were cars on the freeway. I thought, *Don't these people know that my father died? Does the sun really have the audacity to keep rising and setting? How can life be going on around me as if nothing has happened?* I couldn't understand how people were smiling around me. I truly never thought I would ever smile again.

At first, the grieving process was disturbing, downright scary at times. I would be drifting off at night, then have the jolting and haunting image of my father's cold body in a drawer at the mausoleum. I felt like I needed to run down there to be with him so he didn't have to be alone in that cold, dark place. As the days and weeks passed, I began to sleep again but still felt physical pain in my heart when I thought of him; it felt like someone was literally squeezing my heart. I stayed in this phase for several months, and then it was time for the holidays. Are you kidding me? I could not believe that Christmas could actually happen without my father. Christmas *was* my father.

I feel lucky that I got to have my dad until I was thirty-one, but I definitely had moments of feeling it was unfair that many of my siblings were well into their forties and fifties when he died. Sometimes I felt like I received the short end of the stick. However, now that I am ten years removed from his death, I feel that I received just as much benefit from having a good father as my older siblings did. I think about him now as I learn to be a good mother to my son. I think about how caring and nurturing he was to all of us while, at the same time, maintaining a strict line between parent and friend. My father was thought of by our family as the "benevolent dictator." He could be very funny and charming and often was, but even with his friendly and gregarious nature, he was absolutely and definitively *the boss*. Now when I think about the times I got into trouble with my dad, I am actually able to laugh.

It seems like it took forever, but ever so slowly, the pain and sorrow that I used to feel when I thought about my dad was replaced with wonderful images of his smiling, laughing face. In fact, I rarely cry or get sad about my father anymore. Now, I smile.

Carolyn Leone

CHAPTER TWO:

SAYING GOODBYE

Labored breathing, last rites, and letting go—the last days and hours of a loved one's life. Nothing prepares us for them. Nothing in life prepares us for death. There are no high school courses or syllabi that teach the intricacies of how to watch a loved one suffer or wither or take their last breath.

So when women like me are forced to watch their superhero of a father succumb to an insidious disease, it can be derailing. We must suddenly assume the role of caretaker and muddle our way through a mire of medical terms, prescriptions, and doctor visits. Each day becomes a rollercoaster of emotions as the grief stages begin in mere anticipation of imminent death. We wait for test results and try to stay positive, but meanwhile we wonder, with a pit in our stomachs. *When is it going to happen? How is it going to feel? What are we going to do after he is gone?*

The following essays are portraits of women who have endured this kind of a slow, debilitating loss; they capture the blessing and curse. On one hand there is comfort and satisfaction in squeaking out one last "I love you" yet on the other hand, there is the haunting memory of watching him lose his appetite, his hair, and his dignity. Witnessing the debilitating demise of my father was much more than a daughter should have to endure, but I am unequivocally grateful for the last four months I had with him, hanging out in his den, watching his favorite shows, administering his saline IV, laughing, crying, and telling him I loved him. It was a salty-sweet goodbye.

Let It Go

Racing the grim reaper to my father's deathbed, I read Joan Didion's *Year of Magical Thinking*, the story of the year following her husband's sudden death. I finished it on the plane and placed it in my carry-on luggage beside *Babycatcher: A Memoir of a Modern Midwife.* Nervous and worried as I was, I did not miss the irony: birth and death next to one in another in my black-and-white paisley bag.

My father's friend and companion, Billie, kept calling and telling me to come sooner and sooner. First she said come next month "when your dad is stronger." Then, come next week, come over the weekend, maybe tomorrow. Hoping to go with me to comfort her little girl, despite my parent's divorce, my mother kept asking, "When should I come?" "I just don't know, Mom," I would say over and over. I couldn't predict death. I didn't know how to get there in time to see Dad before he died to say "I love you."

Dad's diagnosis was prostate cancer with bone metastasis. He had been given a six-month prognosis seven years earlier. He believed in the power of modern medicine and in his own optimism, and he often felt well. When he didn't, his biggest complaint was his struggle to walk eighteen holes on a golf course. Sometimes he looked sick. Often, he looked like himself only older. He had been in and out of the hospital many times over the past seven years. It was always hard to know whether or not I should be there.

My girls were little—Caroline, three, and Katherine, only ten months—and I couldn't leave them indefinitely or frequently. The luxury of being a stay-at-home mom is accompanied by the restriction of it. Whenever I left for Texas, my husband, Rob, would have to take time off from work. My mother-in-law might have to drive the six hours to our house, taking time from work herself to care for our family.

I had so little control of something so important. I could control trivial things like the laundry detergent we used or what we had for dinner. I could choose what to wear, when to exercise. I could decide what solid foods Katherine would start eating that day. I could decide if Caroline could drink water from a glass or if we should stick with sippy cups for a bit longer. Something so big, knowing when to say goodbye to Dad—this I had no control over.

Talking to Mom in those days before I flew to Lubbock felt strangely familiar. She lived in Rhode Island, while I had chosen to make my home in Virginia. With the birth of each of the girls, Mom had been desperate to be with us, not ten hours away. When Caroline was born, Mom's presence was a luxury. With Katherine's birth, it became a necessity for babysitting duties. In the discussions leading up to my trip to Texas, I told Mom again and again, "I just don't know. I don't know when I should go." I had said these same words leading up to the girl's births. I could count Braxton-Hicks contractions for hours, my doctor could measure my belly— these were numbers that we could gather, but we could not predict my girl's birthdays. I was, in birth as in death, simply not in control.

After days of discussion and worry, I arrived in Lubbock on a Tuesday to sit and wait by Dad's bedside. In the end, Mom had not come. Billie had called just the day before to say, "Come now." Walking into Dad's hospital room, I met his friend Bruce. Bruce was part of a golf group that included Dad, an overweight priest, a one-armed man, and a nearly blind eighty-four-year-old. These were men who had comfortably told jokes and laughed at and among themselves.

Others had come and gone over the past week. After a short visit, Bruce excused himself. We said goodbye and told him we would call. No one said "we will call when Dad dies," but this is what we meant. It appeared that the hospital had run out of options. Three hours after I arrived in Texas, Dad was transferred to hospice.

Dad woke up a bit on the ambulance ride to hospice. He was able to whisper, "I love you" and to barely pucker his lips for a kiss. It was enough. He knew I was there. Then his pain returned. The last round of medication was no longer working. As soon as we arrived, the hospice nurses began administering one pain killer after another. It seemed like enough to sedate an elephant. Dad kept fighting, kicking, turning, and trying to get out of bed. All this was enough to keep me in denial. If anyone could come out on the other side of this, it would be Dad. I began to arrange a ride back to Billie's house to freshen up, maybe sleep for a few hours. Nadine, the nurse, told me I shouldn't go. This was when I began to get it. I was preparing for days of sitting at his bedside, but it appeared that it would be only hours.

I left Dad's room long enough to use the bathroom, brush my hair, and wash my hands. I had left Richmond that morning in the dark, and dark had fallen in Lubbock. I yawned and pinched my cheeks, looking for color in my tired face. I walked back in to meet Dad's minister, Reverend Haney. My dad, whom we had dragged to church throughout my childhood, had found religion after his diagnosis. I would come to realize that the church had kept him alive—perhaps literally but definitely figuratively. His church family was his support, his hope. This night, Reverend Haney performed Dad's last rites. He ended with the Lord's Prayer, which had become Dad's favorite. I continued to make comments about probably needing to give Dad his last rites more than once. Trying to joke, trying to get everyone to agree that he would pull through one more time. Somehow, I let it escape me that as close as we had gotten in the past, Dad had never been to hospice. No one had read last rites. This was it.

I stood by Dad's bed with Nadine and Billie. Nadine said to my dad, "Just let go, Arthur. Just let go. Breathe into it. Your time has come. It is safe. You are safe. Your family loves you. You have done all you were meant to do. Just let go." She knew that Dad was a religious man, so she lured him to heaven, tempted him with visions of the pearly gates. "Let the breath go. Just let go." Dad fought her. I had watched vial after vial of painkiller being pushed into his body. How he moved, I will never know. He pushed and pulled, tried to sit, to roll, his body and his mind fighting the inevitable.

As I stood listening to Nadine, I was shocked, not by my father's impending death but by Nadine's words. Only ten months earlier, Katherine had been born to this same refrain, "Just let go." I had labored easily on that Monday in April until the end. When I came close to pushing, my labor stopped, and Stephanie, my birth doula, began to talk. She knew I was scared to push. This had been the hardest part of my labor with Caroline more than two years before. A movement that should come naturally was hard. I was scared it was going to happen again. "Just let go, Stacey," Stephanie had said. "You have to let your body take over. Breathe into it. Just let it go. Relax. You are safe. Rob is here. I am here. You are safe. Let it go." Finally, I could fight nature no longer. My baby would come despite me. My body knew what it needed to do. "Just let go," Stephanie said again and again. After three short pushes, Katherine entered the world, her calm eyes looking up at me, her small mouth moving, her tiny fingers resting in mine.

Standing by Dad's bedside, I was pulled from my thoughts.

He had calmed down, but he held on. I was exhausted. I had to go back to Billie's and rest. I climbed into Billie's car, following Reverend Haney, who had agreed to lead me along unfamiliar roads. I let myself into a strange house and collapsed on the nearest bed I could find until the phone rang. After a few moments, I realized where I was and rushed to answer it.

Billie told me that I should come. I ran to the car and backed out of the garage, knowing I had no idea how to get to the hospice. I had never been to Lubbock and had barely paid attention as I followed Reverend Haney a few hours earlier. Fortunately, Lubbock is painfully flat, and the hospice was one of the tallest buildings in town. I found my way by keeping the building in sight and driving toward it. I drove the wrong way down roads and looped back to an exit that I had missed. I'm sure I grossly exceeded the speed limit. My dad was a stickler for safety. I kept hoping he would understand.

As I approached the hospice, it started to snow. Snow in Lubbock is rare. Dad had always hated the weather in Lubbock; too much humidity and too little snow. As the snowflakes covered the windshield, I knew that Dad had died. Minutes later, I rushed into his room. Where there had been struggle before I left, there was only calm. Dad lay still on the bed, no movement, no fight, no breath. He had let go, had let nature do its work. He had left the world. His eyes were closed, his mouth had stopped, and his strong fingers were at rest.

Days later, I returned to Richmond, to Rob and my little girls. I cleaned and sorted and organized. I jumped back into my life. While completing the chores of the day, I began the challenge of explaining death to Caroline. I also thought constantly of how Katherine would never remember my dad, how she would know him only through pictures and stories. This little girl, who entered the world to the same words that her grandfather left it, would never know the man. In my mind, though, Katherine and Dad would always share something important. Together, they taught me the struggle, the importance, and the inevitability of letting go.

Stacey Loscalzo

The Blurry Day

It was time.

My dad had been sick for some time, and there had had many close calls before, but somehow I just knew that it was his time.

I mindlessly threw my stuff in the car and drove two-and-a-half hours before I wondered, "Did I change my underwear? Put on deodorant? Brush my teeth?" It was too late anyway. All I could do was hope for the best and use a breath mint.

I lived a hundred and eight miles away and made it to the hospital in just over two hours. When I arrived, my mom was sitting there. She hadn't left the room all night or day. She looked tired and scared but strong. *Is it possible to be all three?* I wondered. *Sure it is. Just look at her.*

As Dad lay in bed, unconscious and laboring to breathe, I sat next to him and started to talk. Here's what I remember about that conversation; it plays in my mind like the first monologue in my junior high drama class.

Hi Dad! Guess what?! I got a new car yesterday. You would like it, I think. It's a Subaru Legacy LT. I'm not sure what the LT stands for, other than it was a special-edition model. It has the all-wheel drive we need for the snow but still has the pep that you would appreciate. It has a sunroof, too. No, it's not your Dodge Hemi.

There was a pause in his breathing, and the corners of his mouth curled up with a half-hearted smile, then there was an uncomfortable pause.

On my way down here, I couldn't even remember if I brushed my teeth or put on deodorant. Please forgive me if I smell funny. Oh yeah, I know your comeback, smell more than usual?

Another pause.

Hey Dad, you know, Tyler wishes he could be here. He understands why he can't and wants you to know he loves you diiisss MUCH! I do too, Dad. Love you, I mean. I hope you know that. I know we had our struggles. Ah hell, we had some fights that were doozies, but none of that matters now. We all love you. I know you're tired, Dad. You've held on for so long. You don't have to be strong for us anymore. You don't. You do what you need to do, and we'll take care of the rest.

Choking back tears, I looked at Mom. I was amazed at what she'd been through: almost fifty years with this man, a man who was not always the easiest person to get along with but sensitive in a way I could appreciate only as an adult.

One of my sisters showed up, then my brother. We all started to converse about small things, all the while trying to pretend we were not caught up in the moment we were in. *Anything* to pretend we were in another place, another time. It was decided that Mom needed something to eat and needed to leave the room even more. Dad had been hanging on all night, and there was no way of knowing how long he would continue. I had two more sisters on the way.

My oldest sister took Mom down to the cafeteria for some soup while my brother and I sat there with Dad. We made small talk for a moment and then just sat there quietly staring. I found myself watching Dad's chest and listening. It sounded like bubbles were filling his chest. My brother and I looked at each other as the breaths became slower and farther apart.

My brother suddenly stood up. "I better go get Mom!"

There I was, alone with Dad, holding his hand. I reverted to the monologue.

Hey there, big guy! You doing all right? I'm here, Dad. You're not alone, you know. Mom's not here, though.

I gave his hand a gentle squeeze.

I know Dad. It's okay.

His breathing stopped.

Dad?

I pressed the nurse's call button at least twenty times.

DAD?!?

A few nurses came in. One ran to him, and one held me. Somehow, it was like the last air bubble popped and escaped from him, and I hoped I was wrong but realized I was not. Devastation hit.

It was his time. He was ready; I was not. I felt like an eight-year-old girl who wanted nothing more than to sit on her daddy's lap and have him tell her it would all be all right.

The next thing I remember was my family at the door.

The rest of the day became a blur. There was some paperwork, sprinkled with meaningless words. Nothing was stopping those last moments from playing in my mind. I'd shut my eyes and see the last breath.

Part of me felt bad for a while. Why had he left with me there? Mom waited with him for so long, yet he went when I was the only one there. Maybe, though he knew how strong Mom was, he didn't want to burden her with that memory. Secretly I think he might have waited for her to leave the room. It wasn't because he and I had any closer bond than he had with any of my four siblings; he loved us all equally. It was just that he couldn't go with her there.

That image has faded, thankfully, and it has slowly been replaced by better memories.

I take solace in knowing that I am not alone. If all women must face this type of loss at some point in their lives, then let me embrace them when they join our club. I will be there to remind them that they are not alone.

I will be there with a box of tissue, a bottle of their favorite beverage, and a pillow for punching, or throwing, or screaming into, or just crying into until they need it to sleep. I will remind them that the pain will fade. It won't go away forever, but it will fade.

Oh, and on the day, the fateful day that your world is rocked to your shoes, that day will become a blur. It won't even have to be a medically induced blur, it will just blur. You will forget what you had for breakfast, whether you changed your underwear, and whether or not you brushed your teeth. It won't matter anyway.

Mary Grandy

Father Falling

When like a weighty stone, my father fell,
smashing the glass he held in his alabaster hand,
fell, with a groan and "Oh fuck,"
fell like a planet out of orbit,
fell out of reach,
fell swiftly,
streaking the air with alarm,
burning a hole in the sky on the way down—

fell with finality,
fell like snow in April,
white and trembling and cold,
drifting, pale,
faded like a late summer lawn—

fell out of the world
like falling out of love,
abruptly—
snapping off branches,
ripping chunks of swollen bark as he fell,
strangled for air,
crumpled like leaves
under the foot of sudden winter,

fell, like brittle bones,
pearl-gray flesh, out of his own fragile skin,
fell quietly,
like ash, like mist, like night
crept up on darkness like a dumb beast—

he fell gracelessly,
losing everything on the way down.

When my father fell, like words on deaf ears,
disconnected, broken-wired,
blue and numb and sagging,
dragging down the globe at the seams,
raining down, spilling over the curved rim,
unable to save himself from ruin,
from abandonment—
fell from ego,
fell from language,
fell into shadow,

fell irrevocably—
from recovery,
from recriminations, accusations,
justifications, rationalizations—

fell, like a wild orange sun
squeezed behind the horizon,
phosphorescent, neon scarlet juice
down to the last molecules
halting like red lights,
synapses detouring,
he unspooled
from the flaring pulse of his own tangled veins,
was shaken loose
from the threads.

When my father fell,
he dissolved in the shapeless surf,
was swallowed,

washed clean of breath,
became immeasurable, as grief—

like emptiness—
grasping the space
where he once stood
haloed in the dying light.

Lori Landau, written for her father-in-law

Thy Will Be Done

I was my daddy's little girl. He raised me as a single dad from the time I was fourteen until I was married. I am so glad I had that one-on-one time with him. My sister wasn't so lucky; she stayed with Mom after the divorce.

Dad was a lover of art, antiques, history, politics, and religion. Funny, those are the things I love today. He always told me how, when he was young, he had been invited to work in Italy as an apprentice to an unknown painter, but my grandmother wouldn't let him go. I remember the funny little cartoons he drew for us with his odd little characters. Froggy was my favorite. All our birthday, Valentine's Day, Christmas, and Easter cards were handmade with Froggy as the central character. Froggy was a sappy little guy who always had so much love to give and so many jokes to share. Dad told stories through his characters and cards; each holiday card was the next chapter of his love story for us. Looking back, I wish I had kept them. They were an expression of who Dad was inside: sappy, with a sense of humor, a goofy romantic. That was my dad.

Dad died six years ago of sepsis of the liver, alcoholic cirrhosis. He was sixty-two years old, too young to go. There was a lot I still had to learn from Dad, a lot of questions I had for him but never had the courage to ask. He was an alcoholic. He was in bondage and couldn't break those chains. I believe he is finally free of the pain he tried so hard to hide through his humor and his drinking, pain from the abuse he endured as the child of an alcoholic mother who shattered his dreams. The alcohol took him over and eventually took his life.

When Dad died, it was a strange day. I had been with him day and night from the moment he was admitted to the hospital a few weeks prior. On this particular day, I had driven two hours away for an acting gig I had been cast in, one I had originally turned down but that he insisted I take. He said he'd still be there when I got back. During the filming, I had an overwhelming feeling of dread and knew I had to get back to the hospital.

I left the set and drove faster than I had ever driven in my life. When I arrived, my sister and mother were there with him, crying. My sister said that he was waiting for me to get there. He had been in and out of consciousness, and she told him to wait for me, that I would be there soon. In that moment, I deeply regretted taking the job. I immediately took his hand and began to apologize for not being there. Something came over me—I will never forget it—I began to pray with my dad. I wasn't a Christian—I had doubts as to whether or not God even existed—but I began to pray. I asked him if he wanted to accept Jesus Christ into his heart. I began to tell him about heaven and eternal life. I asked Dad to believe in Jesus. It was so strange—I was crying and praying a prayer I had never prayed before.

Our Father who art in heaven, hallowed be thy name . . .

I went on with this prayer that I don't recall ever having said before. By the time I reached *Amen*, Dad was gone. I was holding his hand, looking into his eyes and praying when he died. I didn't know where the prayer came from, but I did know that my dad was gone.

Immediately afterward, I had to sign papers, drive home, and make all the arrangements. I was the executor of the estate, so I had to handle everything from lawyers to pensions to estate sales to insurance. It was all too much to handle, so I shut down emotionally; my grieving had to wait.

I had to keep my promise to my dad, "Take care of your sister, she's not as strong as you are," because he was right; she was a mess. I had to be strong and make the funeral arrangements. He wanted cremation and a small service. He asked us to scatter his ashes in the bay that he loved so much. I looked into it, and though it was illegal, we fulfilled Dad's last wish anyway. Early one morning, we went down to the bay with his ashes, a couple of surf boards, white balloons, and orchids, his favorite flower. My brother, my sister, my husband, and I paddled out into the middle of the bay—it was the first week of February and man, it was cold. We said our goodbyes. We released the ashes, balloons, and orchids and just sat there watching the balloons float away. It was so peaceful and quiet, a beautiful silence.

After a year of dealing with all the legal issues, I was finally able to grieve. I think I cried for a year straight. I didn't think I would ever stop crying.

I now live with my husband and kids in the house my father grew up in, the same house I was raised in—first on weekends, then with Dad full-time until I was married. Now I can watch my children grow up in the home that my father loved so much. Sitting at my desk, looking out into the bay where we scattered his ashes, I still see him here with me, literally. My daughter, Stella Elisabeth, is his spitting image, a beautiful blonde with blue eyes, just like his, in a family of brown-eyed brunettes. She has his expressions and mannerisms as well. I think her birth, in addition to living in Dad's house, has helped me cope with his passing. Every room I enter holds a memory of him; I look out the window and see him in the reflection in the water. At dusk, I remember sitting together to watch the sun set over the bay. Every day is a struggle not having him here, but every day, when I look at my daughter, it gets easier, realizing that he has never left me.

Oh, and that unprecedented praying on his death bed? A few years after his death, I became a Christian and it all began to make sense. I realized that I would have struggled later in life, thinking that he was not with God, if I had not prayed with him that day, if he had not accepted Jesus as I do now. I thank God when I think of that day, and I know now that I never lost him. I will see him again, and he will finally get to meet Stella in her time.

Fabiola Murphy

The Gift of Loss

Inspiration in life comes from many places. Mine came from my father, one month after he died. There was no question that he loved me, but our relationship was tumultuous for most of his life. It didn't help that my parents were divorced when I was a toddler and that for most of my childhood, he was the visiting parent. When I was eleven, my father and stepmother were awarded custody of my brother and me. It was a difficult time for this transition. Hitting puberty in a new school and adjusting to a rural lifestyle with a new family dynamic was challenging.

Those years were filled with hostility and discontent from both of us—there was one argument after another. The tension got worse as the years went by. All I wanted was out! As soon as I graduated, I left our house and began my life as an adult. I attended school in Los Angeles and was happy there. During those years, my father and I enjoyed several good visits. He had also attended college in Los Angeles in the 1950s, and that created a new bond for us. After college, I moved back east and eventually got married, moved west again, and began a family of my own. After my marriage, my relationship with my father seemed to regress; it was almost as if it were stuck in that time warp of my teenage years. Although I worked to fulfill the role as dutiful daughter, the relationship still struggled.

Three weeks before my father's seventieth birthday, I debated what to get him as a present. I honestly didn't know what he'd want. We'd lived apart for so many years that I was out of touch with his daily life. It embarrasses me now to remember how I felt at that time. In the end, I found three Jewish books that I thought he would enjoy. Even after

I chose them, I felt there could have been something more significant than just books for such a big milestone birthday, but no other ideas came to me.

It amazes me how quickly life changes. The day before his birthday, he called with the news that he had terminal lung cancer and had been given less than a year to live. I offered to fly to Vermont the next weekend when he needed some assistance at home. It meant finding childcare for my two small children and traveling across the country with very little notice. Without thinking twice, I knew I must do it. I have always been grateful for that decision. It turned out to be one of the most important times we ever spent together, a true turning point in our relationship. It was a unique and special time for the two of us without spouses, children, or animals. It was a gift, and we both knew it.

The eight months that followed were also a gift. For years, we had struggled to find a quiet time to talk on the phone; I was busy with my children, and the time zone difference created challenges. Often weeks would pass without a phone call. Suddenly, with his terminal diagnosis, we found the time to speak every day. We shared stories, laughed, and made our peace. We both wondered why we had waited for a death sentence to move forward with our relationship. I visited him twice more during those months. My father died on December 1, 2006, the day of my son's sixth birthday.

Many of us believe that people can mentor and guide us only when they are alive. In my case, our relationship blossomed after so many years of turmoil only when we knew the end was near. My father continues to guide me even now that he is gone. Sometimes I hear his voice in my mind, answering thoughts about what to do in a given situation. Our physical relationship has ceased, but a spiritual one is still present.

About a month after my father's death, an idea crossed my

mind. My thought was to perform a thousand mitzvahs—acts of kindness—in his honor. Many of the mitzvahs were simple, little actions like sending a thank-you or get-well card, visiting a sick elderly neighbor, helping return a cat to its home, or changing a roll of toilet paper for the next patron. I also volunteered at a food pantry, in my children's school and within our community. In the end, it was a two-year journey. It not only helped me move through my grief, but it also kept me very connected to my father. I learned valuable lessons about giving and receiving throughout this time. In the two years that I worked to complete my mitzvah project, I often felt that my father was guiding my experience.

Grieving a loved one is very difficult. It may be harder and more complicated when that person is someone you have struggled with in life. There can be unease and regret at how your life was lived. I know that if my father and I hadn't had those months together when he was dying, my experience of his death would have been very different. I expect that there would have been a great deal of regret and much more sadness about together-time that was lost when he was alive. I know there would have been more anger to work through if I hadn't had certain conversations with him before he died. I continue to be grateful for the gift of his death and the opportunity it allowed us to find our peace.

When I think about my dad now, I remember stories of good times, long buried under years of bad memories. I prefer to think about the time we had together when we knew he was dying. It was an honest and open time, a time to forgive and move forward, a time for love and light to fill our conversations. This journey of life and death has many lessons. I know I have learned some of mine, thanks to my dad.

Linda Cohen

CHAPTER THREE:

THE CALL

While I was in the process of compiling stories for this book, a family friend got the call no one wants to receive: her father had been killed by a drunk driver. When she and I spoke about the possibility of her writing a piece for the book, she pondered it sincerely but then told me, "Mary, I can't write it down. If I write it down, that means it happened." We locked eyes, and all I could do was nod. I could sense that she didn't want to "go there," so I simply replied, "I totally understand."

Though I could empathize with her pain and feelings of denial, I realize now that there is a part of her grief I cannot fully understand. She did not have a few months or weeks, or even days, to prepare for her dad's death. She was blindsided, adding another weighty layer to her sense of loss.

The women in this chapter can relate to the shock of "the call." They all lost their dads suddenly and were left with questions unanswered and words unsaid. Their fathers were taken from them in a matter of seconds, and they had to process the life-altering news with no cushion of time or space. They had no closure of a final goodbye to aid in moving forward to the next stage of life, and their grief process began just as abruptly as the unexpected call came in.

Four Missed Calls

I was thirty-four when my dad passed suddenly from a heart attack. He was sixty-three. I'll never forget the night it all happened. I couldn't sleep, anxious about a presentation about hearing loss that I was to give the next morning to a large crowd. I'm an audiologist thanks to the support from my dad. As a single mom with two little children, I couldn't have achieved this without his help. I was nervous about my presentation because, although I knew what I was going to say, I didn't want to mess up. I hate speaking in public.

It was 4:00 am, and something in me told me to look at my phone. Four missed calls from my mom.

I called her immediately, and she told me Dad had been rushed to the hospital—she was on her way there now, he would be fine, she'd call me back when she found out more information.

I panicked and waited for her to call me back, and waited, and waited.

Somehow, I missed another call from her. I listened to the voicemail.

It doesn't look good . . . Dad doesn't look good . . .

Then the phone dropped.

It didn't disconnect the line. I could still *hear* everything. It was as if I was meant to hear it.

I heard the heart machines go from a steady beating sound to a flat line and then, total quiet.

I heard the doctor tell my mom that there was nothing else he could do.

I heard him call the time of death: 4:45 a.m.

He asked who they should contact.

Then there was silence, as if the world stopped. My world stopped. This couldn't be happening. I had just talked to my dad. He was healthy and happy.

It was then 5:00 a.m., and my boys, ages three and six, were sleeping soundly. How would I tell them their grandpa was gone?

I couldn't think straight. I knew I had to get the boys to their daycare so that I could help my mom. I am an only child, which to this day is difficult for me, so I didn't say a word to the boys, figuring I'd get to that later.

I proceeded to my mom's house. She was on the couch, slumped over, in total shock. Her phone was ringing off the hook. The news had spread.

I took the phone calls, one after another, explaining that we were just as shocked and, yes, we'd be okay.

My mom answered the next phone call. It was the coroner's office. She started to talk and then sobbed and muttered, "Please talk to my daughter."

I took the phone, and the woman at the coroner's office was extremely sympathetic. She wanted to know if we would donate any parts of his body for research. My dad was big on education and research, so I obliged. We donated his tissues including his eyes and lungs. I later received a letter regarding the research that was conducted and smiled. I knew my dad would have been proud to contribute to these studies.

Immediately after my dad's passing, I experienced a few coincidences that made me wonder if my dad had had a hand in them. My mom's archaic computer gave me no problem while I was typing Dad's eulogy and printing out photos for the funeral, but as soon as I was finished, it crashed and hasn't worked since. I ran errands for my mom prior to the funeral and all my receipts ended in the same numbers: $22.22, $33.33, $55.55. The shoes I found for the funeral were a perfect fit and the last pair available in my size. I was in need of a new car, and my dad had just recently bought a new SUV. My mom thought it only made sense for me to have it. To this day I still drive his car. Were these just coincidences, or was my dad looking down on me, letting me know that he was still there?

I believe we all grieve in different ways. I continued to work and take care of the boys, to keep going. I had many moments when, out of the blue, I'd start bawling. It still happens, and, of course, it's always at the most inappropriate times. I continue to thank God for having my dad in my life as long as I did. I'm thankful that my boys grew up with him and can still remember him; I hope that never goes away. I always wonder: if I had an opportunity to talk to him one more time, what would I tell him? I would definitely want to thank him for being an awesome dad and for teaching me so much, but deep down I believe he's watching and smiling because he sees so much of himself in me. I am my father's daughter and will always be so proud that he was my daddy.

Mika Inouye-Winkle, Au.D., CCC-A

A Father's Love

My father, Eric Charles Thompson, was the kind of guy you'd want to have dinner with. He was funny and entertaining, the life of the party. Part of his charm was how humorous *he* thought he was. I miss hearing his rumbling laugh, a laugh so loud it could be heard across the house and probably clear to the neighbors' houses. This is how I will remember him, laughing hysterically at his own jokes.

My dad was a caring, loving, compassionate man. His code of ethics was comparable to that of the Boy Scouts. He was not published, famous, or wealthy, but he was an ethical, responsible, self-made businessman who was living the American dream. My dad showed me the value of hard work and friendship.

Some of his greatest friends were canines, those lost ones he found homes for and those with homes he doted on. His last earthly gift to me was my puppy. From the moment I saw her, a beautiful Shih Tzu/Maltese mix, I finally knew what the fuss was all about, the unconditional love that melts the heart. Little did I know that this gift (who I named Abigail, which I later discovered means *a father's love*) would get me through the hardest part of my life. She would make me smile and remind me of my dad's love.

As happy as my dad was, he also had a dark side that ultimately led to his death. About seven years before he died, he realized he was struggling with depression. He recognized his anxiety and sorrow, which did not seem normal, as symptoms, so he was tested and found that he had an inactive thyroid. He was put on a regimen of medication that he was told would continue for the rest of his life. Most of his friends and co-workers never knew he was on this medication or that he struggled with depression. If he chose to disclose this personal information, it would have been to help someone in the same situation.

For the seven years that he took medication, he was joyful and happy. However, around Easter of 2008, he began feeling blue again, explaining it as anxiety related to his only little girl, me, likely moving across the country to Boston for law school. My dad worried about my safety, especially being so far away. This is not to say that he didn't want me to move. He was just being a protective father.

On April 13, 2008, he went to the doctor and was given an additional prescription to ease his nerves. As he began taking the medication, he told my mom and me that he wasn't going to let it beat him. We never doubted him. His anxiety seemed to be fading, and he was excited for my mom and me to travel to Boston to look at law schools. She and I left with a certain peace, knowing how excited Dad was for me. I remember giving my dad a huge hug goodbye and telling him "I love you," not knowing that it would be for the last time.

My mom and I left for Boston on a Monday. My dad's brother and nephew saw him that day and remembered how happy he was and how excited for his own dad's surprise birthday party, which was set for the following weekend. What my dad never lived to find out was that the party was also for him. He was just shy of fifty. My mom and I spoke to him on the telephone on Tuesday night, and we shared our last laughs. On Wednesday afternoon, in the middle of Boston, my mom and I found out that my sweet dad had taken his own life.

We have been led to believe that a chemical reaction in his prescription medications caused him to take his own life. My mom and I, our family, and friends know in our hearts that something must have happened, something must have snapped. My dad would never in his right mind have left this world willingly. To think my dad will be remembered for how he took his life pains our hearts deeply.

There was never a moment in my childhood when I didn't feel loved by both my mom and dad. My dad could always make me laugh. In the years just before his death, we had grown closer; our bond was remarkable. He gave me the support, the strength, and the love I needed to get through college. He loved our little family so much, and I know he still does.

My dad taught me many life lessons, most importantly to be a feminist, to stand up for what I believe in because I can create change. He honored his mother by wearing a breast cancer awareness hat and putting a pink ribbon on his truck. He led by example.

I am now in my first year of law school in San Diego, not Boston, and am living my dream, the dream that my father would want me to fulfill. Every day, I wake up to the realization that he's gone, yet a part of me knows he's always with me and will be with me wherever I go, whatever the future may hold.

Here's to my father, Eric Charles Thompson, in tribute to the life he led and the loving father he was and will always be.

Heather-Ann Thompson

Reflections on My Father, Fifteen Years Later

My father died suddenly on March 29, 1993. He had a massive heart attack. He was sixty-five years old. I was eighteen. My life would forever be altered in ways that I couldn't begin to imagine at the time.

I was a freshman in college at the University of San Diego. It was nearing spring, and I was full swing into the second semester of my college freshman year.

In the middle of the night I heard a knock on my dorm room door; I groggily opened the door and saw my brother standing there with my resident assistant. I was disoriented and thought maybe I was dreaming. I could tell something was wrong. He told me that my mom had gone to use the restroom at the end of the hall and would be right back. I was so confused. My brother had been estranged from our lives for many years, so to see him there on the doorstep of my dorm—a dorm with a no-boys-after-eleven rule--was making my brain hurt.

"What happened? What is wrong?" I remember that I asked him several times, but he kept trying to deflect until my mother returned from the bathroom. I must have gotten hysterical in my questioning, because just as my mother was coming down the hall, he gave me an answer. I wasn't prepared for this in my half-asleep state.

"Dad's gone."

"What?"

"Dad's dead."

"What?!!!"

I think I collapsed onto him. This memory is not clear. I just know that I was rocked in my soul. I wasn't thinking clearly, and yet I was overly efficient. I think they expected me to go home with them to my mother's house right away. She lived forty-five minutes away. I insisted on staying in my dorm and told them I would get a ride home the next day after I had a chance to speak to my professors. I had a sleepless night. My roommate was not close to me and was therefore unable to console me, and my dearest friend, Julie, was off campus for the night.

I lay awake in bed, thoughts racing through memories and every conversation, every moment that I could recall of my father. My brain was overloaded but with computer-like efficiency—I felt it filing, analyzing, sorting memories of my now-dead father.

I called my boyfriend, my high school sweetheart, at around five in the morning to tell him the news. It was comforting to share the news with him, to speak the truth out loud, to have him listen as I cried. His simple words and just knowing that he loved me brought me some comfort. Because we shared this, I still hold him in a very special place in my heart. He loved me through losing my virginity and through losing my father.

When the sun came up, I showered and washed the tears from my face. I made my way to the sink to brush my teeth. For the first time in my life, I realized how physically painful tears and sadness could be. My forehead, eyes, cheeks and jaw, all the muscles in my face hurt from crying and grimacing and grieving through the night. Julie found me at my sink. She hugged me and cried with me and helped me to get back to my room.

That morning: visits to professors, looks of shock and sadness. Packing for a funeral in Pennsylvania. Nothing to wear.

Julie loaning me a royal blue and black-checked wool blazer.

My father had moved back to his hometown about a year before at the insistence of his younger second wife. They had been married for only three years. His departure from California, where all of his children as well as my brothers and sisters lived, was a surprise and came too soon, way too soon. We longed for him to be closer to us, and now we had lost him forever.

I don't remember getting to Pennsylvania, although I know we all did: my four sisters, my two brothers, and my mother, who was clearly devastated by this loss. She had been married to my father for twenty-five years and had seven children with him. He was the love of her life.

I remember being at the funeral home for the viewing and the anticipation and fear of knowing that I would be seeing my father in his casket. His hair was so white, more so than the last time I had seen him, which was in August for my sister's wedding. His eyes were sewn shut and seemed misshapen— he was a cornea donor. His lips were wide and flat. He seemed heavier than he had been. He had the aroma of formaldehyde, chemicals, death. Overall, he looked like Milton Berle.

This was, and was *not*, my father.

Whatever had animated him in life was gone. This was the first dead body I had ever seen, and it was abundantly clear to me that there is a God who breathes life into our bodies, that our bodies are merely shells for our souls. This gave me some small comfort. My dad wasn't *here* anymore, and he certainly wasn't *there*, in that body, so I imagined that the essence of him was still *somewhere*.

My father always had a pack of Doublemint gum in his pocket. When we wanted to have a piece, he always tore it in half, keeping half for himself or giving the other half to one of my siblings. Before we closed the casket, each of us tore a piece of Doublemint in half, kept one half for ourselves and placed the other half in the breast pocket of his burial suit. Then we doused him with Brut cologne.

There was a twenty-one-gun salute and a presentation of the flag. My father was a career marine, a master gunnery sergeant, retired from the military before I was born.

After the funeral, I returned to school, dove back into my studies, and finished the school year with straight A's. I believe this is just as my father would have wanted.

This is how I dealt with his death then: overly efficient, overachieving, skipping over some of the important parts of grieving to be able to function day to day.

I never saw a grief counselor or went to any grief group or mourning meeting;

I just dove back in.

It is only with fifteen years of perspective that I can look back on that period of my life and wish I had taken more time to properly grieve the loss of my father. Instead, I have grieved over time, stumbling on the way and picking myself up along the journey.

Losing my father had a devastating impact on my relationship with men. I went through a series of failed relationships that were passionate and dysfunctional. I can't say that I was aware of this at the time, but I was seeking *him*, seeking that strong male figure, seeking someone who would care for me and make me feel protected, loved, and safe. I dated men several years older than me because I was attracted to some quality in them that, I can now say, was somehow helping to fill the void that my father left. I was messed up, it's true, especially on the inside, where it counts.

Through that series of failed relationships, therapy, self-help books, and most of all through time, I have been able to gain some distance from the pain of loss. I am still gaining perspective. As a bride, I had to deal with the absence of my father as I walked down the aisle to my groom. As a mother, I had to come to some kind of peace with the idea that my father would never be here to meet his little grandson. I am now even more motivated to keep his legacy and memory alive so that my son will know and understand who his Papa was.

As an adult, I feel a profound sadness at the loss of my dad. Now that I have a greater capacity to love and understand, I am saddened at not being able to share this time in my life with my father or to reciprocate the love he gave me with a grown daughter's heart, mind, and soul.

In my dreams, he is still alive and has come to visit me on numerous occasions. In my dreams, I spend time with my dad. I learn new things and get to share them with him and show him how far I have come in life.

My sweetest, most tangible treasure from my father is a book he gave me for Christmas in 1990: *The Prophet*, by Khalil Gibran. This is the inscription on the first page.

Dear Laura
May the beauties of life fill your heart forever
Love,
Dad

This book has given me so much comfort and joy over the years. It's been instrumental in my healing process and in my ability to *live* life and live to and through each of the milestones in my life without my father. When he died, I didn't fully grasp the wisdom or sentiment that my father had. I gleaned that over time, through reflection and especially when I read passages of the book he gave me.

I think my father is proud of me, of who I have become, and of where I am in life. I am reassured of his presence by his dream visitations and when I look into my son's eyes.

My father is always with me.

Laura Lee Juliano-Henson

Heart Attacks and Thursdays

I wanted so much for him to recover,
to see me dance across the floor in my chiffon dress:
then pridefully beam
like daddies do
when their daughters desperately strive
to please them.

I wanted him to forgive the indiscretions from my youth,
the ones that planted barriers between us spawning unkind
words.
I wanted to reseed the past—
to run into his arms and say
"I'm sorry."

I wanted to drive to the beach and rest at his favorite spot
so we could ride with the capricious tide
that flowed through his veins.
I wanted to relish everything he loved,
all that he lived for.

I wanted to forget the times he hurt me
and let anger dictate his more sensible judgment
and start fresh like a toddler out of diapers:
to wash the stink of pain
absolve his fallibility—
his audacity for being human.

I wanted to cancel the date of the heart attack,
the one that would forever mar his trust.

Leaving him angry and tormented and bitter,
questioning God and existence and me.
I wanted to jump directly to Friday
and pretend Thursday never was.

Dad survived his "Thursday" heart attack, and initially we
were thrilled. My sisters and I envisioned traditional spaghetti
dinners and visits with our father; we had more time. What
we never planned on was the condition Dad's heart would be
in following that wretched day. The damage was so bad that
his immune system was severely compromised. His body was
unable to fight off the multiple infections that ravaged his
newly emaciated frame.

During this ill-fated time, stuck somewhere between life
and death, Dad grew unhappy and resentful and bitter. He
lived in this unfortunate state for six months. How I still wish
we could have jumped to Friday and pretended that Thursday
never was.

Cheryl Sommese

Truth in Healing

It was 4:10 p.m. on New Year's Eve, 2003, and I had walked in the door from running errands to hear my phone ringing. It was my brother, Neal. "Did you hear the news?" His voice sounded off, and I knew it was bad. I said, "What?" He said, "Dad and Gayle are dead." I wrote it down as he said it, as is my habit to do when I know something important is being relayed to me, something that I may need to remember later.

He shared the details with me. I wanted to get off the phone with him and talk to my mom. The room felt like it was spinning. I felt like I was spinning. My cat was running around the room . . . spinning.

My dad, Bob, and stepmom, Gayle, had died from carbon monoxide poisoning in their home. There had been a terrible storm that knocked out their power; they had a generator in their garage, hooked up to their refrigerator. The fumes from the generator had leaked into their home while they slept.

The next few hours and days after the phone call from my brother were intense. I was on overdrive. I don't recall really breaking down or crying. There would be time for that later.

A friend once told me that planning your parent's funeral is the saddest day in your life. She was right.

The day of the memorial, my brother, Larry, and I were the first to arrive. We were to make sure things were set. Finally, something I could really focus on. We were advancing an event. All of my years of event planning kicked in, and I was on fire. This is something I knew how to do. Where was the food to be set? Are there outlets for the coffee makers? Where are the utensils and napkins? How would the service flow? Do we have music? A mic? I don't think the small-town funeral director had ever seen anything like me before. Poor guy, I meant to apologize later, but I am sure he had encountered worse than a focused event planner.

Once my event planning duties ended, reality hit. A friend once told me that when her father died, she cried for five days. I cried for seven.

Grief is physical. I kept telling myself that if I allowed myself to feel this, eventually the pain would ease. If I let the tears come, eventually the ache would pass. The pain was intense. I have had a broken heart; I have had someone that I love say goodbye. I thought that was pain, but this is real pain—deep in my gut, deep in my soul pain.

Though my dad was part of me, he was not an easy man. He had a loud voice, harsh words, and a quick temper. He also had a quick wit, a great smile, and loved to have fun. My brothers and I all have a good sense of humor and are witty. We get that from him.

Now that my dad is gone, who is going to tell me the story of picking me out when I was adopted? Who will tell me that it was like picking out a puppy? He loved to tell me that story, and I loved hearing it. It was a special story that he shared with me. A part of my memories and a part of my heart are gone.

I kept the note that I had written in my wallet for months after my dad died. I would read the words "Dad and Gayle are dead" and realize that it must be true.

A friend once told me that the sharp knife of grief becomes dull with time. She was right.

The grief is always there, but it does get better.

Tracey Adams

The Circle of Life

The first time I learned of my father's poor health was when I received a call from my stepmother, Catherine, saying that my dad was in the hospital and would be going into surgery. As she shared the series of events that had occurred, I could hear the uncertainty in her voice. "We were just finishing up with a nice dinner and about to have some desert when your father began complaining of a stomach ache. We waited a while, but the pain became too much for him to bear, so we went to the hospital." Apparently my father had been diagnosed with diverticulitis, a medical condition that affects the walls of the colon.

Catherine said that she would call me as soon as she knew anything. I set the phone down and felt my stomach move and was reminded of my daughter's presence within my womb. Tears began to streak my face as I began to consider life without my dad. I contemplated going to be by my father's side but, because I was in the final trimester of my pregnancy, the airlines would not let me fly, and the drive would take too long. I felt so helpless and frustrated by the challenges that stood in my way. The only way I could find comfort was through meditation.

After many updates, I received the final call from the hospital. Catherine said that he had still not woken up from the surgery and that he was unable to breathe on his own. The doctors said that even if they could save him, he would have to wear a colostomy bag and potentially need assistance with breathing for the rest of his life. She felt that my father would not want to live that life, and it was time to let him go.

As I heard those words, I began to sob; my heart ached in

a way I had not felt before. At this intense rush of emotion, I was again reminded of the life growing within me. I stopped the tears and numbed the pain in fear that I would hurt her, that my sadness was too heavy a burden for her sweet unborn soul to bear.

Weeks went by, and I remained in a state of numbness and disbelief. I could not grasp that my father would never know his granddaughter, that she would only know his memory. I could not comprehend that I would never see him play with her, laugh with her, or hold her in his arms.

My deep connection to the Divine, and knowing that my dad and I had gone through intense levels of healing in the last years of his life, were the only things that kept me from falling apart.

On the day of his funeral, everything seemed surreal; I found normal things like breathing and speaking to be quite challenging and awkward. After a heartfelt service and hearing many wonderful stories celebrating my father's life, I decided to step away from the group to reflect on the moment and on the life that my father had lived. As I looked out over the rolling, golden hills, a graceful hawk caught my eye, and in that moment I heard the voice of my dearest spiritual teacher, Deepak Chopra. His words brought peace into my being as I was reminded, "Nothing ever dies, life never ends, and life, like all things, simply goes through cycles."

At that moment, I felt Stella kick. I placed my hands around my belly, and I knew that my father's death was only one part of the cycle and that within me I carried the other piece: life.

Alisha McShane

A Hometown Hero and a Wandering Introvert

When my grandfather passed away, an article in the *Sun Advocate* stated, "Helper, Utah has lost a local hero." I wonder if the reporter knew the full truth behind that statement. As Pa passed quietly in his sleep, surrounded by his four children, seven grandchildren, and four great-grandchildren, along with every significant other, we celebrated his life, told stories of his past, shared our best-loved memories, laughed, and then cried as his favorite tunes played in the background. His funeral was a beautiful traditional Catholic ceremony, the church filled with mourners, all of whom he had directly impacted in one way or another. Our family stayed together, held hands, sang along to *Ave Maria,* and comforted my grandmother, who had to kiss her husband of sixty-eight years goodbye as he lay peacefully in his coffin with his rosary, eyeglasses, and beloved harmonica. It's been only a month since he died, but in that time, I have started going to church more often, I feel more strongly connected to my family, and I look at his picture every night. I pray to him now when I pray to God, knowing that he is looking down on me.

Pa's death was a time of grieving but also a time for celebrating a truly wonderful man. Pa is the second family member I have lost in my twenty-seven years. My dad was the first.

Unlike my Pa, my dad was not much of a family man. He divorced my mom when I was two, and then proceeded to travel all over the world. He held prestigious positions in large corporations, always had nice cars and the latest gadgets, and treated me to fine restaurants, even before I knew what a salad fork was. He thrived on financial success though he didn't want to be perceived that way.

Through all his travels, and much to the surprise of many family members, my dad always made it a point to keep in touch with me, whether it was flying me to visit him in the various cities he inhabited or flying my friends to Puerto Vallarta for spring break, where he treated us to the presidential suite and endless cocktails. When I visited him at home, we always went to lunch at the same restaurant, and our conversations were that of two acquaintances who really wanted to get to know each other on a deeper level but simply did not know how. After lunch, we parted ways and continued to stay in touch with phone calls or emails every few weeks.

On Thanksgiving morning in 2003, I was at my mom's house, getting ready to visit my dad, when my cell phone rang. A man asked to speak to my mother, and even before my mom said anything, I somehow knew what he was telling her. She hung up the phone and gently told me that my father had passed away earlier that morning. I was shocked and confused. I didn't even know he had been ill. "What do you mean, he is dead?" I flashed back to our conversation the night before when, in a barely recognizable voice, he asked if I could visit him on Thursday instead of Friday. He said he needed to tell me something and needed to see me as soon as possible. Unfortunately, Thursday wasn't soon enough.

I sat on my mom's bed, grasping a pillow and rocking back and forth, suddenly feeling like my life was swirling around me. I was full of regret. My father and I would never have the chance to become closer. I would never feel comfortable helping myself to the food in his fridge. He would never walk me down the aisle of a church, meet his grandkids, or call me "cute stuff" again.

The man who had called was the only friend of my dad's who had known of his condition. Dad had been battling throat and lung cancer for six months before he finally succumbed to illness that fateful Thanksgiving morning. He had asked this friend to keep his condition a secret.

My mother was my savior during that hellish weekend. She helped me take care of all the business aspects of his death. We informed his family, whom he hadn't spoken with in years, took care of the estate, and signed over his remains to be cremated and spread at sea. He had requested no funeral or service of any kind, and we honored his wishes. I made a trip to his yacht to gather a few items by which to remember him, and his friend took care of everything else. I stayed a few days extra in Seattle and then resumed my normal life in San Diego. I returned to work and continued with my social life, and everything seemed back to the way it was before my father died.

Grieving was a slow process for me. I led my life exactly as I had before Dad died. Returning to normalcy allowed me to slowly deal with my emotions and come to terms with the situation quietly, peacefully. I didn't talk to many people about my emotions, because most of the time, the numbness was impossible to explain. Over time, I was able to comprehend my feelings. I began to focus on the memories, which then filled the void within me. I learned how to not focus on the "what might have been" but to be thankful for what was.

My father's and grandfather's actions affect the way I make decisions in my life, though in very different ways. The shocking death of my father taught me to appreciate everything around me. Now I always tell people how I feel about them, and I never go to sleep angry. By watching my grandfather live and die with his family all around him, I understand the meaning of unconditional love. I place the utmost importance on family, and I try to maintain strong values.

Although my dad left this planet alone, I hope he knew he wasn't truly alone, that there were people who loved him, people who still love him. My grandfather, on the other side of the spectrum, left this earth surrounded by love. He knew his family loved him, and they knew he loved them. Even though my dad wasn't able to experience the same type of departure, I can only hope that his days were fulfilling and that he looked back in his final hours to reflect on his life with joy.

Andrea Hickey

Background Music

Today marks one year and a day since my father passed away. I miss him more than ever, and the tears still flow all too easily. He was one of those rare individuals who was loved and admired by everyone, and I always felt lucky to be his daughter. He was my all-time favorite person, a fact that was evident to those who know me. His age group is called the Greatest Generation, and he was a shining example of that.

Dad was handsome, gregarious, book smart (he had a doctorate and was a plant pathologist, specializing in citrus), fun loving, hard-working, honest, inspiring, clever, and so much more. He raised my older sister and me from the time we were ten and eight, after our mother passed away in 1970 following a long battle with Hodgkin's disease. He had to deal with raising two little girls and grieving the loss of his beloved wife at the same time, yet I remember mostly happy times as a child. Dad kept our lives as stable as possible in part by insisting to well-meaning relatives that he could raise us in the environment we were used to, our home, with him as our only parent. Because single parenting was nearly unheard of at the time, he had to convince everyone that he could do it on his own. I think he proved his point.

Dad especially loved hiking in the Sierras near his home in Fresno. At age seventy-nine, he was instrumental in mapping out a section of the San Joaquin River Trail. With his Tuesday hiking group, Sierra Club, and other groups, he hiked a large portion of the Sierra mountain range and took detailed notes and GPS coordinates to write a book on hikes near the Fresno area. Some of my favorite times spent with him in later years were when I got to join him on these hikes, including a one-week, seventy-mile backpacking jaunt in upper Yosemite when he was in his mid-seventies.

During one of his weekly Tuesday hikes with his good friends, Dad almost finished the eight-mile hike despite clear symptoms of a heart attack. Ever the scientist, he always wanted to push an experiment to its limits. He convinced everyone, including himself, that he could finish the hike, and he came pretty close. He died in a beautiful spot at Eastman Lake, across from an area where bald eagles nest. He would have loved to know that he would die with his boots on, doing what he enjoyed so much.

When the father-daughter bond is especially strong, as it was in my case, the loss is particularly difficult, but for me it was amplified even more because he also filled the role of mother for most of my life. It was like losing two parents at once. Ever since losing my mom so young, my greatest fear was losing my dad. I was fortunate to have him in my life for nearly forty-seven years. I miss him terribly and still reach for the phone to hear of his latest adventures or get his advice on something before hard reality hits again. He was the one person who understood me best, quietly applauded my successes, and guided me to make the right decisions on my own.

Life will go on, and I'll make it through this, because that is what he would have wanted and because he taught me to be strong and persevere, but it feels as if things will never be as happy and beautiful as when he was here. Shortly after Dad's death, I ran to the desert to draw strength from the sunshine and peace there and because I feel closest to him and my thoughts when I am in nature. My husband and I stopped at a local restaurant for lunch, and I noticed that something didn't seem quite right. It wasn't just that it was especially quiet from the absence of other customers. I finally realized that the soft background music that usually plays in public places wasn't there. That's how it feels without Dad in my life; things seem to go on as before, but the joy and happiness he brought, the subtle music of my life, is missing. Fortunately, reliving the many wonderful memories of him can bring back the music, if only for a short time.

M. H.

CHAPTER FOUR:

GONE TOO SOON

When I read the following pieces, all written by women whose dads died during their childhood, it was hard for me to imagine being a little girl and having to endure the turbulence of grief, the panic attacks, the out-of-body detachment from reality, and the general fog that accompanies loss. Rather than merely being asked to write cursive or multiply fractions, their innocent minds had to wrap around terms like *heaven* and *eternity*. The age-appropriate questions like what flavor Jolly Rancher to buy or what style backpack to use were replaced with "why is my dad not here to tuck me in" and "who is going to teach me how to ride a bike?" Their simplistic childhoods were thwarted by the complex nature of grief.

As the women in the chapter attest to, the grief process for a child who has lost her daddy is a long road full of unanswered questions. For many of them, the journey is filled with searching for a father figure and perpetual issues with self-esteem and self-doubt. For others, it is a means to become stronger in their skin and to build stronger relationships with others. Either way, as the youngest initiates into the club, they had to deal with the complexities of grief before they were able to understand or articulate what they were feeling. Through their stories, they take us back in time and try to make sense of it all.

What If?

I lost my father when I was four years old; an age when un-derstanding death is not possible. All I knew was that one day my dad was there, and one day he was not. Struggle as I did, according to my mother, the reality simply did not register on the mind of a four-year-old.

I was simply too small for the situation, in every respect. Instead of attending the funeral, it was thought best that I should spend the afternoon with family friends. Looking back, I am sure it was the right choice for a child my age, but as a teenager, I asked myself, Was it? Why wasn't I there to say a final goodbye?

As I ponder the emptiness of growing up without a father, two words rise in my mind: what if? What if understanding death was something a child could do? What if he had been there to take me to the circus, what if he had been there to teach me how to ride a bike, or soothe my first broken heart, or be at my graduation, cheering from the stands, or walk me down the aisle on my wedding day? What if? What if he had been there to hold my hand when my mother died? What if he had been there the day my son was born? How would it have felt to hand him his first grandchild? What if?

The void created by his death was vast. As I dated my way through my twenties and early thirties, it didn't take a genius to figure out what I was doing. It was Freud 101. I was look-ing for a father figure, not a boyfriend, and who could live up to that? No one. It took some therapy to recognize my pattern with men, and I finally came to terms with the bigger issue. I had a gap in my life. The absence of a father in my life left some permanent scars on my psyche.

Every child's birthright is to have two parents. Fortunately for me, my mother made up for the loss of my dad. I saw her struggle as a single parent raising two small children, and I know she tried to make up for the fact that he was not there. She would simply borrow a family friend for me for the father-daughter days and make sure that I didn't want for anything in that department. Thinking about those days, I feel a tightness in my throat. Did I ever think about how it was for her to be raising two kids on her own? It sure was easy to feel sorry for all of us, and I did.

In retrospect, I realize that we do the best we can. Sometimes we are handed terrible circumstances and are left to pick up the pieces. What I think we have in common as women is that we are survivors. Our mothers instill that in us from day one. I hope I can instill that in my own son. My worst fear is that something will happen to me before he is old enough to remember me, as I was too young to remember my father.

As I struggle through the early years of motherhood without my own parents to guide me, one thought resonates in my head daily: *What If?*

Ramona Gearin

Monsters

My dad died when I was ten; that was nearly thirty years ago. I remember him as kind, hard-working, and funny. I can remember his smile and certain looks he would get in his eyes. I can remember certain moments vividly; unfortunately, there is a lot I simply cannot remember.

The last years of his life he suffered from cancer, and the ensuing treatments often had adverse effects on him. One particular evening after chemotherapy, he could not sleep, and he asked me to make him some tea. Though I was terrified of the dark at only ten years old, I of course offered to make it for him.

I turned this memory into a monologue in my one-woman stage show called *Little Eve-Finding My Voice*. In this scene, "Eve" talks to her dead father on one of her weekly visits to his gravesite, recalling her desire to help him despite her desperate fear of the dark.

There is another memory I have . . . it is pretty vivid. It was ten at night. Nine years oldv. I was still up, always a night owl. You were up because you had had a bad chemotherapy treatment that day, and you were really sick. You asked me to make you some tea. Instantly in my head an alarm went off, "But the kitchen is dark, wherever it is dark, monsters live. I can't go into the monster-infested dark kitchen." Of course, I didn't say anything, I just stared at you with extreme panic flowing through my body. However, I knew I had to do it—you needed your tea; that was more important. I had to battle the monsters in exchange for you. If the tea was going to make you feel better, then, well, okay.

I looked into the dark kitchen and peered right and left, and then I ran across the dark kitchen to turn on the light. Of course, the light switch was across the room. My heart was pounding. Okay, I survived. I started to heat up the water. As I waited for the water to boil, you waited in your chair, our chair. I kept looking over my shoulder. The kitchen was light, but the family room now looked even darker, and let's face it, the monsters ran in there. They were watching and waiting. I could hear them. I lived through it. I wish I could say the same for you.

I remember this because I have always had a great fear of monsters. I guess I also thought that I was a bigger "monster target" without you living. I mean, it is a universal fact that monsters will never try to fight a dad. When you died, I had to sleep with the closet doors shut so that they wouldn't come out. I tucked my hair under my head while sleeping so that the evil witch under the bed would not cut it off during the night.

I still fear monsters. Obviously, they come in different shapes and sizes now: a big challenge, a tough situation, other family members, a mistake, the monster of fear itself. My own fears are perhaps my biggest, most constant monsters. However, like that night, I face them because of you. Even though you are not literally here, I have learned to believe that you are always with me. That night, you needed me to do something for you. Now, I feel you letting me know that you are with me when I face whatever monster I am dealing with. I want you to know that, 'cause when I say I carry you with me always, I truly mean always.

That's all. I'll see you next week. I love you.

Laura Bozanich

I Was a Girl Named Gegi

The fan blowing from the floor vents did little to cool the heavy, stale air in the Pampa, Texas library. Sitting beneath the sign proclaiming "No food or drink," I guzzled water from the liter-size bottle I'd smuggled in. My throat closed as if I'd gulped a handful of sand, and my stomach curled into a ball as though hiding. I felt like hiding, too, but I was determined to face the truth.

My sweaty hands shook as I threaded the microfilm, so nervous I spooled the film right off the roll and onto the floor. After fumbling for fifteen minutes, I finally got the film threaded properly and began frantically scrolling through *The Pampa News* headlines of 1984. Images zipped by like a movie on fast-forward, and I had to slow down to make sure that I caught each frame.

There it was, on the bottom of the front page, the headline spreading across four columns: "Former Pampa 'Bad Boy' Didn't Have Time to Prove He'd Changed." After twenty-four years of being forbidden to read about my father, I'd finally unearthed the article about his murder.

The story of my father's life, I was told and I had believed, was that in 1976, he joined up with two brothers and they robbed a Pampa five-and-dime; during the robbery, an officer was shot in the arm. They all ran from the building, but the two men sped off in a car, leaving my dad behind, and the police found him sitting in an open field near the robbery scene. It was as if he was just waiting for the law to find him. During a two-year trial, my dad testified against the brothers, but he was still sentenced to a prison term. My mother, my brother Jack, and I followed him to Missouri in the summer of 1978.

While we were in Missouri, my mother struggled greatly as a single, twenty-five-year-old woman with two young children and a husband in prison. Jobs were scarce, and she strained to stretch her paycheck. She was a cashier at a small grocery store, where she was forced to pass a weekly pricing test or lose her job. The longer we were in Missouri, the fewer visits we made to see Daddy in prison, and, in the fall, my mother gave me the crushing news that they were getting divorced.

In November, Jack and I went to live in Pampa with Mimi and Papa, after my grandparents convinced my mother to let us stay with them while she got on her feet financially. We welcomed the kitchen cupboards full of our favorite snacks and Mimi's meaty, home-cooked meals. Living with my grandparents meant I missed my mother, but I did get to talk to and, eventually, see Daddy, my favorite person in the world.

I knew my father as the handsome man who cooked my favorite spaghetti dinner, taught me how to play checkers, and let me help him fix his motorcycle. Daddy was tall, but he was also burly; with his curly, dark hair and tattoos, he could look intimidating, especially on his Harley. His special nickname for me was Gegi, which he created when I was learning to say my name, Jesaka, and kept pronouncing it *geg-ee-kah*.

Daddy was released from prison in 1982, and he moved to Austin, a changed man. When he visited us in Pampa for Christmas, he was no longer troubled and angry. He donated his brute force to a domestic violence shelter, accompanying women as they moved out of their homes to leave their abusers. Daddy told me about standing between angry boyfriends and husbands so that the women could gather their things and find safer places to live. I was proud to have a father who helped keep women safe from mean men.

During that Christmas visit, he spent the entire day playing Clue® with my brother and me, eating M&M's® and WHOPPERS® malted milk balls, his favorite candies. We also visited Daddy during the summer, driving from Pampa to Austin with our grandparents. Jack and I each spent one evening and night with Daddy. On my visit, Daddy spent several hours helping me find old Olivia Newton-John albums in packed record stores. He told me about seeing her in concert and saving his ticket stub for me, but then he lost the souvenir when he was mugged in a park. Daddy said he gave the muggers his wallet and told them they could do more with their lives than steal. I promptly announced that he needed to come back to Pampa. He said he couldn't, and my grandparents insisted it was best that he stay in Austin.

On his last Christmas visit in 1983, I played Willie Nelson's version of "I Will Always Love You" on the piano for my dad. While we were still sitting on the bench in front of my old upright, he told me the story of meeting my mother at a party meant to be his send-off to California, where he was going to live with Mimi's father. When he saw my mother, he was instantly smitten—he told every guy at the party that they had better not ask her to dance but then was too chicken to ask her himself. She once said she couldn't figure out why no one would ask her to dance at the party. He finally did ask her to dance and, a short time later, married her.

On June 19, 1984, my daddy was dead.

Nine-year-old Jack and I had been lolling about on a lazy summer afternoon, watching cartoons with our cousins. Mimi and Papa had been on the phone for a long time, and then they called us four kids to the big kitchen table. My youngest cousin, Becca, only six years old, sat on Mimi's lap while Jack, Maggie, and I filled in our usual seats. Once we were assembled, my grandparents said something to the effect of, "We have some bad news." I don't remember anything between taking my place at the table and landing face down on my bed, screaming, at the other end of the house.

The eight days between the news of Daddy's death and his funeral were a blur. Jack and I were shuttled between my aunt's house and family friends while my grandparents were in Austin to gather Daddy and his things. As soon as they returned, our small house was filled with people and food. We kids sat in the living room, offering quiet, wide-eyed hellos to the stream of sad faces pouring through our front door; my grandparents received guests from their chairs at the kitchen table. Even with the TV on, I could hear my grandmother in the kitchen, her heavy voice ringing above our cartoons, "I went to Austin, then I flew home with my boy in a box on my lap."

No one ever called me Gegi again. Everything changed that summer, and one of the biggest changes was that my grandfather would no longer share *The Pampa News* with me. Our daily ritual was that I would fetch the newspaper from our yard each evening and bring it to the kitchen, where we would argue over who got to read the front section first. Now, I was banned from both the newspaper and the TV news. I struggled to understand what was happening around me and why information was being kept from me. The phone rang constantly, and I overheard snippets of conversations, frequently utterances of "I can't believe they can write that" and "I'm calling the reporter."

A few days after the funeral in late June, Mimi let me read one paragraph of a newspaper article, holding the paper in her wrinkled hands. I was disappointed, as it told me what I already knew, that my father was robbed and killed by his next-door neighbor. Before she could whisk the page away, I managed to read part of a sentence about someone finding Daddy in a car. For years, I imaged my dad's large frame folded into the trunk of a car, and in my young mind, he looked peaceful, as though he were taking a nap.

The last mention of my father's murder was during a night in early August when I slipped out of bed and tiptoed to the living room. Leaning against the wall, I tucked one foot under my nightgown and stared at the TV show Mimi was watching. I heard Daddy's name. The anchor said a man and his wife had been arrested in Amarillo, then she said something about a trial.

"Papa won't be going to that," Mimi said, looking right at me, "he would kill that man."

I couldn't imagine Papa hurting anyone, but I knew Mimi's comment must mean that Papa loved my daddy as much as I did.

My father was not the first child of Mimi and Papa's to die. My uncle Philip, Daddy's younger brother, was killed in a car wreck a few years before I was born. Philip was only nineteen. After Daddy's death, Mimi fell into a long, exhausting, and rarely won battle with depression. Our old house sagged under the weight of so many memories laden with sadness.

She didn't talk much about her sons but on rare, thrilling occasions, Mimi would suddenly share a fond memory with us. My favorite was a story of Daddy and his brother getting in trouble for shooting another kid in the butt with a BB gun. Even though Mimi claimed she was mad at her boys for that, she always told the tale with a big smile. When I was sixteen and asked her to find the old pictures of Daddy, Mimi's dark-brown eyes filled with tears. Although she said she'd try, I knew it was too hard for her, and I never asked again.

Two years later, as I left for college, my grandparents gave me an 8x10 black-and-white portrait of Daddy. My father had always talked about me going to college, even when I was in the third grade.

"Gegi, what are you going to be when you grow up?" he had asked during one of his calls from prison.

"I don't know, Daddy!" I had replied, giggling.

"You need to think about it, Gegi. Where are you going to go to school? We need to start planning."

I started thinking more about my father, about his life and his death, while I was at school, but it was hard to talk about him. While it seemed like everyone in Pampa knew my situation, new friends were curious about why I lived with my grandparents. I found it much easier to simply explain that my dad had died when I was eleven instead of sharing the whole confusing story. Mostly, I just kept quiet about it. Daddy's absence was the most painful as I walked across the stage to receive my bachelor of arts degree. I wished he were sitting in the audience, cheering, as I knew he would have been proud of me in my cap and gown.

I had always missed my father, but the pain intensified after I graduated and moved to Seattle. My grandparents tried convincing me to return to Pampa, but I was determined to be on my own and felt drawn to the West Coast. I felt close to my dad, as I forged my path, exploring the world beyond my family. Still, I ached to talk to my father, curious about his opinion on current events and wondering how he'd like Seattle. He did make it to California after marrying my mother, but their stay was cut short by Philip's death. I speculated that he must have felt free, looking at the Pacific Ocean and living thousands of miles from his parents. Although I'd dreamed of living in a big city since I was young, I wondered: if my dad were alive, would I have chosen to live so far away from him?

While I wanted my father to be with me in the present, most of my questions about him, his death, and his life, concerned the past—they lay dormant, sometimes nagging but mostly just quietly occupying space. As Papa and then Mimi passed away in 2004, their bodies worn out by a lifetime of smoking and tragedy, curiosity about my father grew. I suddenly realized that I could dig up my father's past, my past, without causing my grandparents distress. It was a painful freedom.

A family gathering in Pampa, which I did not attend, prompted my youngest cousin Becca to contact me. She had been the six-year-old sitting on my grandmother's lap the day we learned of my dad's death. Becca was now thirty, and she wanted answers, too. I was thirty-five, the same age as my dad when he died. As we talked about our shared family history for the first time, Becca asked me about my father. When I confessed that I desperately wanted to know what happened, she revealed a story I had never heard. In her version, men looking for Daddy's next-door neighbor shot him by mistake. When the men realized that they had the wrong person, they had taken him to a church and left him there.

That story didn't match my faded image of Daddy in the trunk of a car. This version was gentler, but was it true? Had my father been left at a church to die? Did someone help him, or was he alone? Was he on the church steps, or was he inside? Who found him? These images played as an endless loop in my mind.

I burned to know the answers, to learn exactly what had stolen my father from me twenty-four years ago. I wanted to learn more about him and needed to know what my grandparents had hidden from me. With lots of stomach churning and trepidation, I turned to the Internet and began searching for my father. My sleuthing turned up nothing, but I did manage to get a copy of my dad's death certificate. When I finally received the document in the mail, I was struck by seeing my grandfather's angular signature. He had to sign this document riddled with blanks, and "unknown" filled the space for time of death. The cause of death was "apparent gunshot wounds." As gut-wrenching as it was to see this form, I couldn't begin to imagine my grandfather's pain as he bent his six foot four frame to sign that awful document, his furrowed brow casting a dark shadow across his brilliant blue eyes.

After receiving the death certificate and pausing to restore my courage, I finally admitted to myself that I knew where to find the answers: *The Pampa News*.

During a visit to Pampa, where my brother, now thirty-two, and his young family had settled, I headed to the library one afternoon, claiming that I wanted to find some old articles I'd written in high school. I was scared about what I would find and wasn't ready to make it real by discussing with my brother.

On that afternoon, with the fan feebly blowing stale air, I found it: "Former Pampa 'Bad Boy' Didn't Have Time to Prove He'd Changed." The information was both shocking and oddly satisfying. I was a little disappointed that my cousin's version of my dad's death was not true. I guessed that someone told her that because it seemed easier for a child to understand. The truth was that my dad was shot and robbed by his neighbor, most likely for drugs, and then left near a creek outside of Austin and found a few days later by a hiker. He wasn't in a car; a sheet of tin, weighed down with the seat of a car, covered him. The reality was far more gruesome and painful than Becca or I had known.

That was not why my grandparents forbade me from reading the local newspaper. What I discovered was that my dad had been mixed up with the wrong crowd from an early age. He was stuck in a cycle of law-breaking and redemption. Despite his love for Jack and me, he couldn't break the downward spiral of drugs and destructive decisions. In 1975, shortly after my brother was born, Daddy started driving for my grandparents' trucking business, and it seemed like he'd finally adapted to being a responsible parent. Drugs and two brothers proved to be the beginning of his undoing.

What I learned in *The Pampa News*, more than thirty years after the crime, was that my dad did rob a local five-and-dime, and the brothers did leave my dad at the scene, but these three men had first broken into a guard armory and stolen a cache of automatic weapons. About one month later, the threesome returned to the armory for a second robbery, and it was then that a police officer was wounded by one of the brothers. The five-and-dime robbery occurred in April, 1976, four months later, and the gun my dad used in this robbery tied him to the armory thefts.

The mean, foul-mouthed, ski-masked criminal portrayed in the newspaper was not the funny, gentle man I knew. My father clearly turned his life around after prison, and that fact makes me proud to be his daughter. Although I couldn't confirm my theory with my grandparents, I figured that they didn't want him to move to Pampa because they were worried about retaliation from his testimony against the brothers. I wonder if Mimi and Papa initially thought his death was related to that. It must have been reassuring and, ultimately, more heartbreaking to know that his murder had nothing to do with the trouble he had been in the 1970s. I especially wondered if Mimi thought she could have protected her eldest son if she'd let him move to Pampa.

There is still so much more that I want to learn about my father. The old newspaper articles painted the worst possible picture of him, and I love him anyway. To unearth anything else about his life would be a treasure, much like the one picture I have of me with him. I'm not sure how, or if, I'll ever find answers to all my questions, but I know I am ready. Though I miss him terribly, I am so thankful to know more about the man who called me Gegi.

Jesaka Long

Telling Eileen

My father, Paul Yoxsimer, died of a brain aneurysm in January 1974. He was thirty-one years old, a lieutenant in the sheriff's department, and the father of four. I was six years old. I am now forty-two, and when I tell people that I lost my father at such a young age, a common response is, "Well, at least you were so young that it must have been easier." Not at all. If anything, the loss of my father has become more and more acute as I have grown older. With each milestone in my life, I have been aware of his absence. I wrote this poem entitled "Telling Eileen" when my son was six years old.

Her hand was sweetly soft
marshmallow candy in mine

I dared not squeeze too tightly
(dappled brown braids)

Standing under the tamarisk tree
I squinted
and said
"My dad died"

"I know"

oh

everything sticky and messy
sweet marshmallow candy

bare feet on concrete
drive

soft and hard
soft and hard

her soft brown braids
my hard-plaited blond

the sun melting
everything away

BethAnne Yoxsimer Paulsrud

"Telling Eileen" first appeared in *Literary Mama* in May 2006.

The Woman I Am Today

In this moment, as I'm grasping for memories of my father, I glance at a photograph of him that hangs on the wall. He's standing next to a British guard in front of Buckingham Palace, a place I visited a couple of times during my early years of travel. The photo was taken in the mid-eighties; I was about five years old when he left for six weeks on a historical trek with my mother's brother. It was the trip of a lifetime for him, and I remember missing him. I was so anxious for him to come home and tell me about his adventures so that I could imagine myself one day experiencing the mysteries he had uncovered.

I was seventeen when my dad passed away in 1997, just as I was beginning my senior year of high school. My brother was thirteen. The death of my father inspired me to branch out socially, after a few long, lonely years of shyness. I realized that I needed more people around me, all kinds of people, even those who were considered a bad influence, to help me get through the grief. I learned about myself through them because at that time, they were all I had and all I wanted.

The fondest memories I have of my dad are the times when our similarities were revealed. He'd admire my drawings of far away places and Disney characters, and we'd read books together about astronomy and history. I'd sneak into his office over and over again and stand in awe of his historical memorabilia as if seeing it for the first time. We'd build LEGO® pirate ships and fortresses together, for my younger brother's pleasure, of course. He helped me save money for my first trip to France and England when I was a sophomore in high school. He was always interested in my studies, no matter how much I wanted to avoid them as a young teenage girl. He was just like me in every way. Two years before the photo on the wall was taken, when I was three years old, he almost died from colon cancer. I knew him for fourteen more years before he passed away from stomach cancer at the age of forty-four.

I often wonder if he felt that he accomplished everything he wanted to in his life. He said he was content before he died, but when I think of my own accomplishments, I think of him and wonder if he still wishes he could share them with me in person. This has been one of my toughest challenges in dealing with my dad's passing: knowing that he would have enjoyed hearing about my travels and experiencing my successes. This makes me sadder than anything, yet in many ways I am comforted by his steady presence during the times I think he is missing. He is truly always there, always observing, supporting, and loving, just not in the way I'd like him to be, not in real time, not in the flesh.

It's interesting how I've met so many women with similar stories about their fathers. We always seem to share the same emotional common denominator; there's nothing that can replace the father-daughter relationship—not a boyfriend, husband, stepfather, uncle, brother, mother, nothing. This relationship is a special bond, different from anything I have ever experienced. My dad and I had the kind of relationship any daughter would dream of.

My dad's passing changed my relationship with my mom. It was a challenge for us to communicate on an emotional level. We were never as close as my father and I were. I always felt that my brother was the cherished one and I was the experiment in her mind. They developed more of the bond while I was the outsider, strong and stoic, unaffected by their closeness, or so I thought. My brother could never understand why I acted the way I did. We all grieved in different ways. I was internally destroyed; my mother and brother were externally emotional and angry. It was difficult to accept that this event would affect me for the rest of my life, but I grieve for him every day. I'm grieving right now.

His death also impacted my relationships with men. My first relationship, at twenty-three, turned into a three-year nightmare. I remember crying out to my dad, often blaming him for my fear of abandonment, which my now very ex-boyfriend used at the time to control me. It was a devastating time in my life, and I lost everything: my independence, my personality, and my faith. I'm still trying to get it all back and have been doing pretty well; I've been single and happy for three years now. My faith in love and trust needs some work, but I feel that once I'm fully confident again in all aspects of my life, faith in love will return, and I hope I will find the perfect relationship that my parents had.

I found that after three years in that first, unhealthy relationship, I had lost a part of myself. Since our breakup, I've raced to get myself back on track, acknowledging my quirks and mistakes, taking on new challenges while accepting who I am without forgetting where I came from.

I truly feel that my dad helped to mold me into the woman I am today. I hope that women who have been challenged with the same issues I have can find refuge in knowing that no matter what, a father's love will be there, always. I love my dad more than this memoir could ever express.

Jody Auslund

CHAPTER FIVE:

MEMORIES AND MEMENTOS

"Death leaves a heartache no one can heal, love leaves a memory no one can steal." Someone sent me this quote in one of the many condolence cards I received after my dad's death. I don't think it had as much impact back then as it does now, when I am many years removed from that time in my life. In the height of my grief, memories of my dad served as painful reminders of his absence, yet now, I glom onto them, for they are all I have left. Though they may morph through time and fade with age, they are still with me at all times, in my reach, in my possession. I can gain strength from remembering how he cheered me on during volleyball games, or I can get a laugh from remembering how he inadvertently passed gas while on a tour through Westminster Abbey. Despite the global takeover of email and texting, I still send handwritten cards to my family and friends on special occasions, because I remember how it made me feel to receive his thoughtful cards. When feeling frustrated, like I can't go any further, I persevere, because I remember how hard he worked to become successful. He is still with me in countless ways.

In this chapter, women capture the essence of a father's love through the memories they hold dear, the memories that shape and sustain them as they move on without their dads.

Eagle Feathers

Fourteen years before my father died, when he was perfectly healthy, he wrote a letter to me but did not give it to me. He tucked it inside a vase in which he displayed several bald eagle feathers that we had collected together in Alaska. About a year later, when I was eighteen years old, I was looking at the feathers and found the note. He walked in as I was reading it and confessed that he had intended for me to find it after he was dead. I suppose he assumed that one day the inevitable would happen, and in going through my parents' things, I would encounter it. My father died nine years ago. Now I keep the vase, with the feathers and the note still inside, on my dresser and read it on occasion. Though he wrote it in life, I interpret it as a message from the other side. I hear his words as though he were speaking them now.

As I clean these feathers, tears come to my eyes. My mind returns to a different time and place—a time so precious yet never to be lived again. Katey was twelve. It was our first experience together—the two of us on an Alaskan adventure together. Everything went so wonderfully. What a bond we developed! Memories are like treasures, but they do accentuate the inevitable passing of time.

These bald eagle feathers were gathered during a grizzly bear search we embarked upon on Admiralty Island, Alaska. It was a gray, drizzly day. We had a wild guide who took us into the remote rain forests wading into rivers, pushing through the dense forests. Bald eagles were everywhere; the rivers were red with spawning salmon, the woods bristling with evasive and invisible bears.

If you ever find and read this Katey, I love you so much! I hope we have a chance to repeat an adventure together like this somewhere in the Universe again.

Dad

I talk to my dad all the time. He still gives me advice, still rolls his eyes at me, and best of all, we still laugh hysterically together. I look forward to our repeat adventure someday, somewhere in the Universe.

Katey Reid

Mother's Day

It was Mother's Day, 1968. I was ten years old: the youngest girl among five siblings, the eldest being my sister Leona, next in line my brother Jeff, then Irene, then me, the youngest being my brother Ray, rounding out the Chemnick clan to seven, not including pets.

When it came to celebrations and special occasions, my dad loved taking lots of time to pick out the perfect greeting card. Birthday, anniversary, Valentine's Day, though I imagine the latter was dispensed with after the third or fourth kid. Even for those cutesy Hallmark-invented holidays such as Secretary's Day, my dad wanted to choose just the right card.

When we were kids and Mother's Day rolled around, Dad wasn't obligated to buy a card as his mother had passed away years before, but he loved watching as the five of us marched up to our mom, carefully holding those precious cards we had made at school—the construction paper, stuck with flowers and other adornments, a bit sticky and still smelling of glue.

Cards were usually accompanied by gifts, the kind of gift you could afford at that age: IOUs like "good for one bathroom cleaning" or "good for emptying the dishwasher for one week." On Mother's Day or Father's Day, I think we were all thankful that the recipients rarely cashed in these gifts.

This Mother's Day started out like any other, but as we concluded the cards and gifts portion of the morning, my father shushed us and announced, "I also have a gift for your mom." The five of us stood there in silence, whether it was because we had been told to shush or because the news took us by surprise, who knows. My mother, who was still in bed on her special day, lay speechless as well. Wearing a secretive smile, dad ushered the six of us out of the bedroom and told us to wait outside while he prepared his gift.

All at once, we were all talking and asking questions. "What's up with Dad? He's acting kinda goofy. Come on, Mom, you gotta know what's going on." The bedroom door flung open, and my father called out enthusiastically, "Come on in, everyone!"

We rushed back in the bedroom, anxious to see what kind of gift our dad would buy our mother. To our astonishment, laid out on our parent's bed were three beautiful suits of varying colors—sea green, deep blue, and smoky gray. Next to each suit, my dad had neatly arranged a matching dress shirt and an assortment of spiffy accessories—ties, cufflinks, even matching socks! My father only wore two colors of socks that I could remember, black for work and white for sports.

For a moment, no one said anything, struck by the sight of not one, not two, but three suits. My father never cared about clothes. Were all these suits for him? Why had he bought all of this stuff? And why was Mom suddenly hugging and kissing Dad?

"Your mom is always wishing that I would dress up, so guess what? She got her wish for Mother's Day!"

My dad wasn't quite finished with his surprise. What came next was almost a bigger shock than seeing the clothes laid out on the bed: he *modeled* each suit, cufflinks, socks, each entire outfit. We watched my shy, soft-spoken father parade out of the bedroom, across the entryway and around the living room in his new suits, as though he did it all the time.

To be honest, I don't recall how much use my dad got out of those suits, or when they were finally given up for good and donated to a thrift shop for a second life, but that's not the point. Those suits were a token of my father's generous and loving nature. He gave us all a gift that Mother's Day—a memory to treasure for a lifetime.

When my father passed away just a few months ago, we recalled dozens of such memories and wondered which ones to share at his memorial. Looking back on that time, I guess it was typical: Family and friends gathering to pay tribute, recalling stories, some funny, some poignant, with lots of food and wine consumed throughout the afternoon, well into the evening.

I would love to have him back for just one day, just one hour, to tell him what I have discovered: You've made a difference in this world. Your kind, loving spirit will live on in anyone who was lucky enough to have known you or, like me, one of five kids who had the incredible fortune and privilege of calling you Dad.

Francine Chemnick

The Music Man

Seven years ago, I lost my father to cancer. Seven weeks ago, I gave birth to my second daughter. Tonight, with the nursery dimly lit, I am barely keeping it together, just as frazzled and disoriented as I was when my dad passed, but now for different reasons— sleep deprivation and raging hormones. As I rock and sing, sing and rock, cradling my newborn, I fade in and out of alertness. Though my eyelids are heavy, I stare at her perfect face, memorizing every curve and angle, so as to etch this blissful moment into the archives of my mind. I am pained a little to think that she will not retain this same memory in her own archives, and even more pained to think she will never get to know my father, but the ease of her breath and the smell of her innocence are euphoria to me. I relish the moment, and we melt into the recliner. My mind drifts away.

As I float beyond reality, I land in a time and place from long ago, one that I have glamorized into a dramatic movie in my mind. I have masterfully crafted and choreographed a two-character show between a man, my dad, The ever-serious attorney, and a one-year-old baby, me, based on stories that have been told to me by my family.

Apparently in March of 1973, I was left alone with my dad while my mom went on a two-week vacation with her best friend. For the few months prior, my parents had been separated, but my dad agreed to move back in while my mom was away. For two full weeks, he stayed with me, alone in the house, with the help of my half-siblings and the housekeeper. When my mom returned from her vacation, rather than moving back out, my dad decided to stay for good. The little girl in me, the daddy's girl, wants to believe that he stayed as a direct result of our two-week rendezvous; that I had won him over with my cooing and adorable smiles. Whatever the reason, I am glad he stayed.

Though I have no true memory of this time period, I can envision my father, all six foot six of him, standing over me in my crib as I babbled and kicked, pooped and cried; I can just see him not knowing what in God's name to do with me. I picture him holding me up to the sky until I giggled and then bouncing me on his knee until I sang. These images are rather comedic considering that my father was such a serious, stoic businessman, but he also had a silly, humorous side that came out every once in a while. In my heart, I want to believe that he cherished this time with me—that he sang to me, played me some ragtime on 8-track tapes and strummed a little Dixieland jazz on his beloved ukulele, all the while feeling nauseous from the smell of talc and spit up yet sucking it up, knowing this one-on-one time with me would be precious and fleeting. He and I were in it together, making it through those two weeks with laughter, smiles, and music.

For the following twenty-eight years, music was our connection; it was our thing. Many of my favorite memories of him have to do with music. When I was a little girl, we performed a duet—something about a barking dog—at family gatherings and parties. Boy, do I wish I could remember that song now. What I do remember was sitting on his lap while he strummed the ukulele that looked like a Cracker Jack® toy next to his mammoth frame, and me, howling like a pup and giggling hysterically. During my school years, I relished our special trips to Tower Records, where he let me pick out anything I wanted, from Michael Jackson to Van Halen. Whatever my musical taste, even when he didn't like it, he supported it. While in college, he and I won a "Name That Tune" game at the Father-Daughter Dance my senior year, thanks to our broad knowledge of music. I still have the handmade puffy-painted sashes proclaiming the Dick and Mary Burt Duo the winners. Toward the end of his life, during his chemo treatments, we listened to the local classical music station on his black Sony portable radio, talking about trivial matters, to keep our minds off the reason we were there.

At a sweet whimper from my little one, I look down at her and smile. Inspired by the memory of my dad, I begin to sing her a lullaby, the first thing that comes to my mind. It's a song from the classic musical, *The Music Man*, one of my dad's favorites. The lyrics flow from my lips with ease, and with them come tears. As I continue to rock back and forth, my mind fast-forwards from the previous scene of me as a helpless but thriving baby to twenty-eight years later, with my dad as a helpless, dying man. This time, my memory is crystal clear.

It was May of 2001, just weeks after I married the man of my dreams. My husband and I had moved into my parents' house to help take care of my dying father. I sat with Dad in his den every day. We watched his favorite movies and TV shows, like *Rumpole of the Bailey* and *The Sting*. We listened to music, usually ragtime or classical. Sometimes we just sat in silence, awkwardly trying to avoid the proverbial elephant in the room. Together, we laughed, smiled, and sang songs.

I recall one night in particular. The room was dimly lit, just like this one. The smell of morphine and death filled the air. Though it made me nauseous, I sucked it up because I knew our time together was precious and fleeting. There was nowhere in the world I would have rather been. He was in a comatose-like state, as he had been for a few days; the end of his life was imminent. I listened for the rattle in his breath. *Is that it? I can't tell.* My mind was playing tricks on me.

To calm my nerves, I did something instinctual, something soothing. I began to sing. I went right to my musical theater repertoire, which I knew he loved because he had been the one to introduce it to me. *The Music Man* was perfect, having everything: patriotism, a love story, a brass section (albeit fake), some good ole' fashioned Gary, Indiana humor, and best of all, a barbershop quartet. There in our dining room turned dying room, I sang to my father. Supposedly hearing is the last sense to go, so I stood there, holding his hand, staring deeply at his face, memorizing every curve, every angle so as to etch the bittersweet moment into the archives of my mind, pained to think he may not even know it was me but hopeful he could at least hear me. I sang:

Lida Rose, I'm home again, Rose
To get the sun back in the sky.
Lida Rose, I'm home again, Rose
About a thousand kisses shy.
Ding dong ding
I can hear the chapel bell chime
Ding dong ding
At the least suggestion
I'll pop the question.

As I sang, I saw his lips move. They were curling, curling up into a smile. He could hear me.

Lida Rose, I'm home again, Rose
Without a sweetheart to my name.
Lida Rose, how everyone knows
That I am hoping you're the same.
So here is my love song
Not fancy or fine
Lida Rose, oh won't you be
Mine, Lida Rose, oh Lida Rose, oh Lida Rose . . .

Tears filled my throat. I couldn't go on. His smile had converted into a grimace of sorts, a melancholy, poignant, clownlike frown. He was sad it was over—both the serenade and his life. I held back the tears though I wanted to fall on his body and weep. I felt like we had shared so much in that exchange.

I will miss you.
I will miss you, too.

With that implied exchange, he sank deeper into his coma and died the next day.

The melodic cries of my daughter bring me back once again. I tighten my hold on her. This moment is overwhelming me. I am overcome with joy at this new life in my arms, yet I am weighed down with grief that neither of my daughters will ever know their grandfather. Rather than cry, I begin to sing again. I pick up where I left off, seven years ago.

Dream of now
Dream of then
Dream of a love song
That might have been.

Do I love you?
Oh yes, I love you
And I'll bravely tell you
But only when we dream again.

I realize that she will know this moment, and she will know my father. Both my girls will know my father through the music, through me.

Mary Burt-Godwin

Butterfly Kisses

On Father's Day in June, 1997, I found the perfect gift that encapsulated my relationship with my father: Bob Carlisle's "Butterfly Kisses." When I bought him the tape, I never imagined that four months later it would provide comfort to him while he lay in the ICU recovering from open-heart surgery. He was blind, paralyzed from the waist down, on life support, and I was 3,000 miles away, attending college.

On hearing the news of his sudden surgery, I immediately jumped on a plane to Connecticut from California, praying that this wouldn't be the last time I would see him. The nurses had warned me ahead of time that he would not be able to see or speak to me. As I walked into his hospital room, I noticed that he had head phones on and was listening to "Butterfly Kisses." As I removed the headphones, the machines monitoring his heart rate were beeping uncontrollably. His heart rate was racing. He knew I was there. Even though he was happy to see me, I knew he would not have wanted me to see him in this state. He was jaundiced and clearly not well. It was as if it was someone else's body with my dad's spirit.

As I stood by his bedside, I noticed that he would turn his head to the side as if he could see me. It broke my heart, but I held back the tears, because I wanted to be strong for him. The only way for us to communicate was for him to raise his eyebrows to a yes or no question: One raise for yes, two for no. I'm sure there was so much he wanted to tell me but couldn't find a way. I knew in my heart that he was telling me how much he loved me. He knew he was going to die.

Shortly after his passing, I was a guest on a nationally syndicated talk show called *The Leeza Gibson Show*. After the taping, a man tapped me on the shoulder and said, "This is going to sound strange, but your father would like me to tell you that he is here, he loves you, and that he is okay." It was as if time stopped for me at that moment, and everything else around me was a blur. My dad was reaching out to me.

It is moments such as this, or the times that I see butterflies in unusual places, that bring me peace. Peace in knowing that he is here, that he loves me, and that he is okay.

"I close my eyes and thank God for all the joy in my life, but most of all for butterfly kisses."
—**Bob Carlisle,** *Butterfly Kisses*

Nicole Boyle Dominguez

Wedding of My Dreams

God works in mysterious ways. I have always thought so, but now I know.

I had all but given up on meeting Mr. Right. I am a teacher, and there are very few opportunities to meet men where I work. I thought maybe I would meet somebody in my master's program, but it was full of women teachers. I tried blind dates and used friends as matchmakers but nothing panned out. I left bars wondering what I might tell my kids when they asked where I met their father.

It was October of 1999. I got an email with an ad attached for an online dating service. That was ten years ago when online dating was unheard of, strange, not done. I was bored one day, so I filled out a profile. No one had to know, right? My tagline was, "Do you have a passport?" Instantly a couple of men contacted me. It was fun for about a week, checking email for responses, writing back, and so on. Then I started looking through the profiles for my perfect match. I found an extra-cute guy who had eaten at a seafood buffet in Macedonia. Who goes to Macedonia? Only someone with a passport! I shot him an email: *Tell me about Macedonia.* A thoroughly detailed account of ShyGuy72's military experience overseas came back, and I wrote back. He wrote back. I wrote back. Then one of us suggested that we talk on the phone. We talked nightly for hours, until ShyGuy—his actual name is Wade—suggested that we meet in person. Though I was worried about ruining a perfectly good thing, I finally agreed. We met for a beer and an IMAX movie. Sparks flew. The more I got to know him, the more I liked him and eventually, loved him.

While all this was going on, my dad was waging the fight of his life. In July of 1999, he was told that he had cancer. In August, he had major surgery that removed two-thirds of his stomach and one-third of his esophagus, followed by chemotherapy and radiation throughout the fall. The surgery and treatments ravaged his body. Formerly a robust man of over 230 pounds, he now weighed 160 pounds. A day whose activities he could once handle with little effort now left him exhausted and bedridden. I tried to spend as much time as possible at my parents' house, visiting and attempting to cheer up my dad.

My mom was out of town for the weekend. I had a date with my dad. It was time for him to meet my "Mr. Right."

Wade and I sat on the floor in my parents' bedroom sharing a pizza and a six-pack while shooting the breeze with my dad. This was the ultimate double date--me with my two favorite men. They hit it off instantly, much to my relief, and I could feel mutual respect and affection developing between them.

Throughout the fall and into the new millennium, we spent lots of time with my family. My sister, Amanda, flew up from San Diego often. My dad had a clear CT scan, the ultimate good news, and was given a clean bill of health in February. Though his pre-cancer energy level never returned, he did find the strength to work part time, play the occasional game of golf including teaching Wade how to play, and take a trip to Hawaii with his bride of thirty-one years.

In July of 2000, Wade and I took my parents to a Sacramento River Cats game to celebrate their wedding anniversary. Unbeknownst to me, while I was in the restroom with my mother, Wade asked my dad for my hand in marriage. A week later, Wade proposed to me atop Twin Peaks in San Francisco in front of two tour buses full of tourists who broke into thunderous applause upon my acceptance.

We set our wedding date for April 7, 2001. I couldn't wait for my wedding—I had been planning it for twenty-nine years! I wanted it all—the beautiful dress, vibrant flowers, six bridesmaids, limousines, a walk down the aisle with my now-healthy dad, yummy food. My dreams were coming true! We had a delightful engagement party. The dates were all set for showers, parties, the wedding rehearsal, the honeymoon, we were ready! We even bought a house and planned to move in in December, before the wedding.

In early December of 2000, my mom and dad noticed that my dad's abdomen was starting to swell. On December 13, on our way home from our last premarital counseling class, we met my parents at the emergency room. While there, the doctors informed us that the cancer was back. I remember asking Wade, "Is this real? Is this really happening?" The cancer was gone ten months ago; he had a clean bill of health. My dad had endured a hellish surgery, chemotherapy, and radiation. The cancer was supposed to be gone, gone for good.

The doctors released my dad from the hospital, and we met with his oncologist who assured him and us that with additional chemotherapy treatments, he'd make it until our wedding day. As we neared Christmas, it became clear that was not going to happen. I vividly remember sitting in the living room of our new house, surrounded by moving boxes and asking Wade, "Are you ready to get married?" Without even a second's hesitation, he said, "Yes."

The following morning, we went to the county recorder's office and got our wedding license. When we told my dad and showed him the license, a look of relief washed over him. Our favorite pastor agreed to marry us on December 24. I didn't have my dress, many of our friends would be out of town for Christmas, no invitations, but our immediate family would be in town for the holiday, and my dad would be there. What's more important?

Our wedding may have been spur of the moment, but I tried to make it as special as possible. I took our rings to an engraver and had them inscribed with our favorite Bible verse. I ordered a bouquet and a boutonniere from my neighborhood florist. Our wedding cake was a replica of the delicious cake we had shared months earlier at our engagement party. Wade borrowed a sport coat from his father. I bought a dress off the rack at Nordstrom; it was navy blue with white polka dots—not exactly traditional but perfect. Ironically, just months earlier, I had lined up everything for our April wedding. It took me weeks to plan what I thought was the ideal wedding day, and now I had planned everything for our December wedding in just three days. Wow.

My dad's health was declining quickly. He was bedridden, and on the morning of the wedding, we were wondering if he was going to be able to make it to the church. I remember thinking that we might have to move the wedding to my parents' house. We finally got him up and into a wheelchair. We draped a blanket over his lap, because his abdomen had now become so swollen that he didn't have a single pair of slacks that fit. We arrived at the church and everything was in place. I was told that Wade was waiting for me at the altar. All of our close family and friends were there. We were set.

Before the doors opened and the processional began, my dad and I promised each other that we wouldn't cry. In the end, my dad could not walk me down the aisle, but he was determined to get me down the aisle, and he did. We heard the music and with my dad's best friend, Paul, pushing him in his wheelchair, my dad got me down that aisle. I remember looking over at him, and he had a very contorted look on his face. For just a moment, I didn't know why he looked so pained until I realized that he was almost gritting his teeth trying not to cry. Both of us made it down the aisle without a single tear.

I was so relieved to see Wade at the end of the aisle waiting for me. As soon as our pastor started speaking, everything around me disappeared. The previous two weeks slipped away, and it was as if Wade and I were the only two people in that church. I can truly say that becoming Wade's wife was the happiest moment of my life. After the wedding, we took numerous photographs with every possible combination of family members, most of them including my dad. It went unsaid that these would probably be his last photographs.

My friends Kara, Alicia, and Julie put together a beautiful wedding reception for us at my parents' house with delicious food, yummy drinks, and best of all, our cake. While we celebrated, my dad drifted off in his recliner in the next room. He had mustered all of his energy to get through our ceremony, and now he had nothing left. He sat motionless while we opened our wedding gifts, trying hard to stay involved in our special day but obviously exhausted. Wade and I were staying at a bed and breakfast in downtown Sacramento for our wedding night, and I remember my sister pulling me aside and asking me if I wanted to be called in the middle of the night should something happen. Absolutely, I said, but no call came that night.

We tried to celebrate Christmas day, but it was awkward at best. We all had presents for my dad, and he would open them and cry. Then we would cry. While we wanted him to open the presents that we had carefully purchased before we knew he was sick again, we knew that chances were almost certain that he would never have the opportunity to enjoy them. At the same time, it would have been more heart-wrenching to have nothing for him to open.

It had become apparent that my dad was very uncomfortable now. While he did his best to hide his pain from us, now that our wedding was over, he was declining rapidly. It was almost as if his will to hang on began to weaken once the important landmark he was striving to meet was past. A couple days after Christmas, my dad's brothers and sisters arrived from back east, but by the time they arrived, he had slipped into unconsciousness.

My dad passed away sometime in the early morning hours of December 29, 2000. One of my worst fears, losing a parent, was realized on that day. In the span of two weeks, I had moved into my new house, gotten married, and lost my dad. What I realize now is that God knew I never could have endured one of the most painful times of my life without the simultaneous joy of starting my life with Wade.

One of the last conversations I had with my dad involved my promise to go ahead with our wedding scheduled for April 7, so we did. He knew how important it was to me. I felt his presence with me on that special day in April, and though it was an incredibly beautiful day, the real wedding of my dreams was our small, impromptu ceremony on Christmas Eve. While there was no fancy white dress and no formal tuxedo, I married my Mr. Right, and my dad was there to share that joyous occasion with us.

Cheryl Barto Chandler

Dad Fix

When my dad died, my body went through physical withdrawal symptoms. I not only missed him emotionally, but my body physically missed him, and I needed to get a "dad fix." We talked on the phone every week, and I really needed to hear his voice. I remembered that I had an old answering machine, the kind with the small tape, and over the years, I had saved many of the special messages that had been left for me, such as the ones with my nieces and nephew singing "Happy Birthday" to me. Though I no longer had that machine, I had kept all the tapes for posterity's sake. I bought a small portable tape recorder and started to review the tapes in hopes that maybe I had inadvertently saved one of his messages.

I found two messages from Dad. One was from when he was sick, I could hear it in the sound of his voice, but the other message was from years prior when he was still healthy and vibrant. It reminded me of how deep his voice always was, rich with strength and confidence. It was so good to hear. It was my fix, the injection that my body needed. It felt like he was still alive, sitting at home in his den, in his favorite chair, calling me for one of our weekly chats. I never knew that something so simple would make me miss him so much yet also help me with my grief.

You never know how much you will miss someone's voice until it's gone.

Jennifer Burt

Homecoming Court

"It's better to be looked over than overlooked." This famous quote from Mae West was one of my father's favorite sayings and seemed to become our family motto. My father, Vic Vine, had the good looks of Dean Martin, the loud golfer's wardrobe of Rodney Dangerfield's character in *Caddy Shack*, and the friendly attitude of Will "I Never Met a Stranger" Rogers. To put it mildly, my father was a larger-than-life character and lots of fun to be around.

In south Texas, where I grew up, high school football is its own religion with the homecoming game being one of the high holy days. Alumni return to cheer for their team, and girls of every age proudly display school loyalty by pinning giant white mum flowers decorated with three-inch ribbons, stickers, trinkets, glitter and pipe cleaners in school colors onto their chests. In 1983, when I was a senior at King High School in Corpus Christi, I was nominated for the homecoming court and had asked my father to be my escort. Before the game, each nominated senior girl is announced over the loud speaker and has the privilege of walking out onto the football field with her escort. Our school colors were green and white, and my dad got into the spirit of things by wearing his "golf course green" sports jacket that looked like he had just won the Masters Tournament. I wasn't crowned homecoming queen that night, but I was bestowed a cherished memory of having my dad beaming proudly at me and feeling the volume of his and my mom's love and pride, which was a very special gift.

Five years earlier, in her mid-forties, my vivacious and affectionate mom had died suddenly, leaving huge holes in the hearts of my father, older brother, sister and me. My father was so heartbroken that ten days after my mom's death, he had a mild heart attack. Fortunately, it wasn't fatal. Like any family wading through the deep muck of grief, those first few months after Mom died were spent trying to find a semblance of normality in our upside-down world.

A year later, my father spun our world a bit more when, after a quick four-month courtship, he married a much-younger, blonder, and less-demonstrative version of my mom. Like my dad, she had three children of her own, and I suddenly went from being the youngest child to being the middle child. Add to this the fact that we were all teenagers, and you can imagine some of the hurdles of this arrangement. Now, thirty-three years later, I realize this blended family limb of the family tree has been a real blessing to my life, but at the time, as a grieving, hormonally challenged, motherless teenage girl, it was a very difficult transition.

I really wanted to be happy for my father and his newfound happiness, but I was too overwhelmed. I was just trying to stay afloat. I felt like I had been thrown overboard into the Abandonment Ocean. I tried to remain hopeful and tread water so I wouldn't sink, but I grew more tired and discouraged as it seemed like no one heard my cries for help. I watched the new family boat sail on without me and disappear into the faraway horizon. The harsh reality sunk in that they weren't coming back. Things had changed—everyone had forgotten me and the way things used to be. I was a small dot floating in a vast ocean with no land as far as the eye could see. I clung to the life preserver of the memory of my mother's love and my life before she died.

With the new family dynamic, my relationship with my father changed. In one swift move, he seemed to have fast-forwarded from grieving widower to carefree honeymooner.

This change made me feel as if, without warning or without saying goodbye, he had left me alone in "I really miss Mom" town. This was a major adjustment. I had lost my grieving partner. Out of respect for to his new wife and children, my father seldom talked about my mom or our family's past. This strategy left each of my former nuclear family members struggling to deal (or not deal) with grieving for mom in our own ways. I was left with a lot of gaps in my life that I tried to deal with as best as I could.

I knew my dad loved me in his own way, but he sure did not win any awards for being the best at showing it or making me feel like a priority. That is part of what made that night he escorted me onto the football field so special. It was one of those rare moments when he openly told me how proud he and my mom were of me, and it felt a bit like getting a fix of my "before Mom died" Dad.

After that night, life went on (as it always does, whether you are ready or not), and it was my turn to enter the college and adult phase of my life. I moved away to college and then out of state to pursue my career. Over the next few decades, I enjoyed seeing my father and the rest of our family every couple of years when I came back for periodic visits.

In my mid-thirties, my father passed away. As I was helping to prepare for the funeral, I went through his home, collecting the photographs that captured moments from his colorful life to display at the funeral. In his office, I came across a photo of my father and myself from that happy homecoming night long ago. As I picked up the photo, I felt something on the back of the picture frame. I turned it over and discovered a small browned, curled newspaper clipping taped on the back. Little did I know I was about to receive a much-needed wink and hug from my father.

Intrigued, I read it.

1968—Easter Royalty—Displaying their crowns and prizes are the four winners of Coral Haven Service Club's Annual Easter Baby Show: Karen Vine, age 2, daughter of Commander and Mrs. Victor Vine, picked as this year's Queen.

My eyes filled with tears of joy as I realized that my father had saved this thirty-five-year-old article from my youth. During that year's annual Easter Baby Show, in all of my toddler glory, I had been christened queen! My heart swelled as I realized that my typically unorganized and unsentimental father had taken the time to save that article from my not-very-well-documented childhood and tape it to the back of the picture. I now have that homecoming picture, with the article attached, sitting on the desk at my home in Texas. Looking at the joy in our faces reminds me of how much fun my dad could be. Although he wasn't perfect, he sure knew how to live life to the fullest and generally tried to have a positive outlook. At this point in my life, having lost both my parents and my fifty-one-year old big brother, I "get it" that life is short. I try my best to celebrate each day, count my blessings, and let people know that I love and appreciate them. I am thankful that I had my father as a mentor. I am often encouraged by that photograph and by the glint in my father's smiling eyes saying, "Go, Karen! You can do whatever you want to do!"

Recently, I decided to see if there might be some inscribed message from my dad inside the frame. My hunch was partially right, because I did discover a nostalgic note written on the back of the photo, but instead of being authored in my dad's recognizable ALL CAPS print, I found the words penned in my own loopy, teenage-girl cursive.

Karen Vine & Vic Vine (Dad!)

Homecoming Game, October, 1983

Thanks for escorting me, Dad!! I love you! Happy Father's Day! 1984

It was another wink, this time from my teenage self, a wink of reassurance that I had expressed my love and appreciation to Dad while he was still alive.

To end as I began, here is another Mae West quote that expresses my dad's flamboyant zest for life, which continues to inspire me: "You only live once, but if you do it right, once is enough!" What a fun and ever changing journey life is! Thanks, Dad, for always inspiring me to live each day to the fullest no matter what life may send my way. I love you and miss you and continue to have lots of fun trying to "do it right."

Karen Vine Fuller

Keys, a Cap, and Other Memories

I grew up with my dad and his parents on a farm. He divorced my mom three years after she handed me to Grandma and walked out. Dad had chosen to stay with his parents after their wedding, even though my mother definitely wanted her own home, which may have been the cause of their troubles. Dad faithfully stayed and took care of his parents until their deaths left him alone. He never remarried.

I have a weird memory of thinking Dad was the hired help and Grandma and Grandpa were my parents. I have no idea where that came from, whether it was wishful thinking or only a mistaken, fleeting impression from a lonely young-ster. Dad was hurting and short-tempered for some time after the divorce. I remember hiding behind Grandma one day in the kitchen because Dad was really mad at me for something. We moved from that house when I was five, perhaps to get away from old memories.

Sometime in my preteen years, I remember sitting with Dad by the upstairs dormer window. I was so afraid of light-ning and thunder—until that night. As we watched the light-ning, he explained how the clouds were building up static electricity. He joked that the thunder sounded like someone had dumped a sack of potatoes, which made me smile and lessened my fears. I think of Dad almost every time I experi-ence a thunderstorm.

Dad and I grew closer as I grew older. He mellowed, and I found more understanding. He taught me to drive, but as with everything else, he was extremely overprotective. If I was driving on the road and a car was coming, he had me pull over and stop until it passed. I was almost twenty when I finally got my driver's license with the help of the young man I later married. Like many girls, I was eager to get married and have a home of my own, and going away to college had more than one purpose. One day as I caught a ride back to college, I happened to look back to wave at Dad, and I got a really good look at his face. That look revealed the pain in his heart watching his little girl leave home. It is a vivid and heartbreaking memory. I saw the same look in his face when I got married. He warned me about my decision, but I was determined to have my own home. Perhaps if I'd listened, I wouldn't have had the marriage problems I had.

For twenty years, I went home to Dad several times a year—to rest, get his precious hug and feel loved again—so I could go back to my marriage and family feeling rejuvenated. Sometimes when driving at night, I can feel the eager anticipation of those visits home.

Dad died of a heart attack at age seventy-five, very unexpectedly, and I was devastated. I lay in bed, awake most of the night, hurting inside from the pain of loss but thankful that I had known such a wonderful father and thankful that he was no longer alone and in pain. For that last year, after a tree fell on him while helping a friend cut wood, he was in excruciating pain. He didn't sleep well, and he worked to keep his mind off the pain. For several months before he died, he was working on his house, getting it ready for me to move in with him after my divorce. After he died, however, I didn't have the inner strength to make the move after all.

His death left me in panic and depression for almost two years. I had found my mother several years earlier, or rather she had found me, but I was disappointed in our lack of real emotional connection. Before he died, Dad and Mother had talked a few times and made their peace, even though Mother had remarried.

The year before Dad died, he rode in the local town parade as Man of the Year. I still have the plaque they gave him. He was a jack-of-all-trades kind of guy, and almost everyone in that small town had used his services at one time or another. One woman, living alone outside of town, called him to fix her lamp. No charge, of course. The local sheriff used him as a sounding board to solve local crimes. Among Dad's things was an old cigar box filled with keys. When Mrs. Brown went away for an extended vacation, she gave Dad a key to watch the place. When Mr. Davis needed someone to fix something, he gave Dad a key to get in and do the work. As it turned out, Dad was the unofficial town caretaker.

The church was packed for his funeral. Mother and her husband were there, which surprised everyone because Dad had never told anyone about her. I remember sitting there, looking up at the big wooden cross that my dad had made as a memorial to his parents. I remember walking out of the church that day with a smile, thinking that no one would probably understand why I was smiling. I knew Dad was now free of pain, in heaven, and that I would see him again someday. It was a spiritual victory. God had given me a strong assurance of His Presence, and I felt His loving arms around me, comforting me, helping me through this time of deep sorrow.

We auctioned off everything that we didn't take for ourselves. Afterward, when everyone was gone, I sat alone on the back porch steps. Looking around, it was so empty, so unreal. Then I noticed his old farm cap over the pole of the clothesline. Navy and cream striped, like an old railroad cap. I had no idea where he got it, but he had worn it a lot while he worked. The front had two tucks to form the top curve, there were two air holes on each side with metal eyelets, one of which was missing, and the back had been re-stitched with a sewing machine a time or two. It was worn and a bit soiled, but it was something I could hold onto for a moment when all else was gone. I still have it, just as it was the day I found it.

Betsy Kelleher

CHAPTER SIX:

SEE YOU IN MY DREAMS

A few weeks before my dad's terminal diagnosis, I awoke in the middle of the night in hysterics. Real tears, real sweat, real panic. My dad's imminent death had just been foretold to me in a nightmare. My once-strapping, superhuman father shriveled into nothingness in front of my mind's eye that night. I told my fiancé, hyperventilating, "My dad is going to die." My premonition became a reality less than six months later.

Ever since his death, I continue to have similar dreams of my father, but now I relish them, whether he's the robust man I knew as a kid or the sickly man I knew just before he died. When I awaken from a dad dream, it takes me a while to readjust to the fact it was just a dream, and then I analyze it. Did his wave from the shore as my boat pulled away mean that he is missing me? If he was reading *War and Peace*, upside down, did it mean that I was making a foolish mistake in my life? Regardless of their meanings, dream visitations always stay with me for a while afterward. Sometimes I want to tell my kids to pour their own cereal so that I can go back to sleep and extend my time with him, because in that state, I get to see his face again, and hear his laugh. His laugh is one thing I miss the most.

In this chapter, women describe some of their dad dreams, with a mixture of comfort and angst. Some are nonsensical, while others are full of wisdom. Either way, it's time with Dad, and for that we don't complain.

See you in my dreams, Dad.

The Torture Chamber

Five years ago, I said goodbye to my dad for the last time. His death was unexpected and sudden, though his final days seemed to last forever. It was not because of the pain or agony or the sleepless nights that week. His last days were filled with enough love, bonding, intimacy, reverence, and forgiveness that they could have lasted forever. During this time we exchanged "I love yous" and "I forgive yous" and even a few laughs. He was surrounded by his family and those who knew him best and loved him most, day and night. As the week went on, he lost the ability to speak and eventually the ability to open his eyes. He still responded with wordless gratitude when I put water on his lips or when his sister lovingly trimmed his nails. He scolded us, too. When our discussions became too heated, our stories too animated, or our laughter too loud, he would, in his own way, tell us to keep it down.

On the final day, after receiving the last rites from the priest, my dad, who had not uttered a word in days, responded, "Thank you, Father." We had wondered if he knew what was happening to him, why we were all there. With those three words, we knew he did; we knew he was ready and that he was at peace. Shortly after that, he opened his eyes and looked at each one of us as if he knew it would be his last time. His eyes were still so blue, with no sign of age or deterioration. Oddly enough, during that week my father appeared to grow younger than his years. His hair gained luster, his wrinkles faded, and his cheeks took on a rosy tone.

As he looked at us, we all knew we were not as peaceful with his going as he seemed to be. We were all together, touching him as we held one another and said our final goodbyes to our dad, our brother, our husband, our friend. He took a few deep breaths, and then he was gone.

I will never forget that his last breath was an inhale. It was as though he went inward, almost as if he were returning to himself.

He died on a Thursday morning. It was as though he planned it that way to make it as easy as possible for us. Since his death was unexpected, we had made no funeral or burial arrangements or managed any of the countless details that death entails. We spent the day in a haze making these arrangements, writing the obituaries, and calling friends.

It was so hard, and so blurred, and so fast, yet it felt like forever, and now it feels like a dream. I can hardly remember it. We did it; we made it through. We made it because we had each other. We had spent that last week with my dad as a family, a unit, and we sent him from this world with the same unity.

I wish the serenity of that week could have continued, because the month that followed was exhausting—necessary, but exhausting. My mother and I took care of my father's affairs. We put his finances, insurance, and debts in order. We took on the daunting and emotional task of combing through every inch of his private space and every item of his personal belongings. I spent days poring over his books, his poetry, and pamphlets for organizations with which I didn't know he was associated. I found movies that I didn't know he had seen, music that I didn't know he listened to. I found his handwritten thoughts on the death of his own father. Until then, I had no idea that the grief of that loss had weighed so heavily on him.

I tried to picture him watching these movies, where he wrote this poetry, what he thought about when he was alone in this space. Did he know that his life would end so soon? His mother died suddenly at the age of fifty-nine; he may have had a hunch, he may have known. Did he plan this? So many thoughts were going through my head. My mother and I helped the other professors plan a memorial service for him at the university where he taught. We provided pictures of his life for the memorial. His life that was already so full before mine even began.

As emotionally draining and physically exhausting as it was going through his things, I was grateful for the experience. It was as though I was given the chance to spend some quality time with his memory during the period when I was probably coming out of shock.

I played the outgoing message on his answering machine again and again just to hear his voice. I had never before given any thought to the voice, the laugh, the sound of my dad or any of my loved ones. The realization that I would never again hear his voice, his laugh, or hear him saying my name, was the toughest and most painful reminder of my loss.

In the months following my father's death, I went through various mindsets and stages of grief. I was only twenty-eight years old and had very few friends who could handle the weight of being around me. Their own fear of losing a parent made them run from my need to talk about it. I certainly didn't fault them for that, but I was having a hard time finding resources to help me explore what I was experiencing. As the months wore on, I began to fear my emotional unrest and feel as though I was going to burst. I couldn't sleep at night. I was having visions and nightmares. The moment of my dad's death played over and over again in my head, and I could not get that visual to stop. I kept feeling as though I could have done more, like he was not okay and I had to get back to him to help. I later found out that I was having a common experience of grief called "the torture chamber." I was trapped in my grieving process, stuck in my torture chamber.

As the moment of his death played in my head every night, I spent my days exhausted, on an emotional rollercoaster. My family and friends started to worry. They knew I was not doing well, and while they did their best to help me, they just did not know how.

I started searching for outside help. I went to see four different counselors, all of whom failed me miserably. They did not know the first thing about helping the bereaved. One of them tried to prescribe medication, the next one was obsessed with how my dad died because she didn't want to die young herself, another asked me about mortgage rates for her refinance, and the last one told me that I had no problems and that I should go to school to be a counselor myself. I found these visits as costly as they were useless.

Finally, a personal acquaintance of mine noticed that I was in a lot of pain and offered to talk with me about it. Unbeknownst to me, he was a non-practicing minister and counselor. Most of all, he was a friend. He helped me so much. He asked me how I was and how I felt, and he asked specific questions about my dad and my relationship with him. He asked what I wanted to remember and what I might like to forget. He took me on a guided memory exercise in which he asked that I describe in great detail my favorite childhood memory with my dad. He was so kind and helpful just by talking and asking questions, by not being afraid to get personal, and most of all, by really caring. That night, when I went to bed and prepared to enter my torture chamber, I fell gently into a deep and much-needed sleep.

When morning came and light filled the room, I awoke slowly and stretched sleepily. My dad was sitting on the edge of my bed, twenty years younger, as he was in my memory.

Dad?

Yes, with a smile and that familiar, sarcastic laugh.

Is it really you? Are you really here?

Yes, with wisdom, with peace. He was calm and smiling.

I reached out to him, knowing it was a dream and that I can't touch in my dreams. He took my hand.

It was him—I felt it, I literally felt his hand. I recognized the touch of my dad's hand. It was so familiar, so like my own, so real. I had never dreamed of anything this real. We held hands.

Dad?

Yes.

Are you here?

Yes.

Are you okay?

Yes.

Yes. Yes. Yes. Thank you.

A noise in the hall caused us both to look toward the door, and when I looked back, he was gone. It was if he came to put me at ease, to appear as he looked in his younger days when I was innocent, to let me know he was okay. It was as though he knew no one in my family could help me except for him, so he came to me—in a dream, or a visitation, perhaps. I have not set foot inside my torture chamber ever since.

I started going to a young adult bereavement group so that I could share my experience with loss and to possibly help someone else in the process. It proved to be more therapeutic than I had expected. All of us were able to come together and talk about our challenges of living with loss in a world that refuses to address death in any real way. Discussing these issues in a group helped me gain some perspective and humility about my own personal experience with death and grieving.

I met people from all walks of life: one lost his little brother skiing, another lost her fiancé in a car accident, several members of the group lost a parent to a long-term illness, and some, like me, had lost a parent unexpectedly. We all understood one another. Our losses were very personal and not truly comprehensible to others, but each individual loss shed light on how to grapple with our own grief.

As I continued to go to the group, new members arrived with very recent experiences. A young man came in just days after his mother had died in his arms at their home. The haze around him was palpable. The fact that I could see it, that I could talk to him, answer his questions, comfort him, and assure him that it would not always feel this way, was proof that I myself had come out of the cloud, that I was moving on from my grief.

Today, five years later, I have progressed so much since my dad passed away. I still have occasional dreams about him— dreams that are always peaceful, always loving, and almost always funny, just as I remember him to be. He often shows up with my dog; my dog's death had a devastating impact on my earlier youth, and even he seems happier now. It's always good to see them.

I am still grieving. Most days are better now, but a day doesn't pass when I don't think of my dad. As I learn and grow as an adult, there is so much I wish I could ask him, show him, and share with him. Occasionally when I'm preoccupied or having an experience I would like to share, I'll get a panicked, guilty feeling in my gut, "I need to call Dad! I haven't talked to him in *forever*!" The memory creeps in slowly that he is not reachable.

The reminder that my dad is no longer alive doesn't annihilate me anymore. Rather, it's bittersweet, a reminder of my experiences in this life, that he made me, that he raised me, and that I am still connected to him. The power and strength that I have gained from the loss of my dad are gifts for which I am eternally grateful. Most importantly, I have a deeper understanding of life and love. I am more accepting of myself and the people and situations around me. Through his life and his death, he has given me this clarity. Of course, I would rather have *him* back, but since I can't, I will cherish the gifts he has given me and hope that the way in which I live my life honors his memory.

Megan Kelleher Palmieri

Watching Over Me

My dad was diagnosed with leukemia on May 23, 1996, a few months before I turned thirteen. He was told that he had three months to live. It was a very special time for me, because I had been studying for a long time to have my bat mitzvah that July. I was hoping with all my heart that my dad would make it long enough to share in this important moment in my life. Unfortunately, he passed away in June.

About a month before my bat mitzvah, shortly after my dad passed away, I went dress shopping with my mom. My parents weren't in the habit of spoiling my brother or me, but my dad had told my mom, before he died, to let me get whatever dress I wanted, no matter what the cost (within reason, of course). I was so excited, although in the end I got a very cute, inexpensive dress. A few nights later, I had a dream that my dad was walking around the house in a coma-like state, as if he had returned from the dead. I asked if he would like to see the dress. He told me he had already seen it, as he had been watching me the day we bought it. I was so excited to know that he had been there! It made me feel like he was definitely watching over me and would be with me for the rest of my life.

Since then, I've had similar dreams about him a few times every year. When I was in college, I had a dream that I was on campus and saw him walking around. He had come to meet me. We continued walking together, and I pointed out some of my friends and told him a little bit about them.

Recently, I had a dream that my mom and I were having a party and my dad was there. I talked to him for a while and then went to find my mom. I asked if she knew he was there.

She said of course she knew; she had invited him. I asked her if she realized that he was dead and had been for a while. She said, "Of course, but that doesn't mean he can't spend time with us."

I find immense comfort in these dreams, though they are bittersweet. When I wake up from a dad dream, I am so excited to have seen him, to have shared a part of my life with him. Then reality hits, and I'm sad to wake up because it means that my visit with him is over. Nonetheless, the dreams give me hope that my dad is still watching over me, sharing in my important milestones.

Jennifer Kalker

Blanket from Above

My dad died suddenly on December 16, 1998. He was only sixty. I was thirty, and it was much too soon for me to lose such an enormous part of my life. He was my best friend. I could call him with any problem, any question, anything at all. He was funny and charming, and he loved his family deeply. He was a huge worrywart. My mom, my siblings, and I would make fun of him because he'd stress so much over our well-being. All he cared about was protecting his family from the bad things in this world.

My bubble burst the day he died. He died before he met any of his four grandchildren. He died before a lot of things. The first question I asked God was, *"Why?"* There were no answers for a long time, but now I know why.

The first year after his death was a blur. The second and third years were filled with oceans of tears, confusion, and questions. The fourth and fifth years were filled with anger; that's when the drinking and drugging started. If losing my father was so painful to me, I couldn't even imagine how my mom felt. Her pain was my main concern, so I was determined to be there for her as a shoulder to cry on, as a cheerleader to lift her spirits. My career requires me to be upbeat and positive, happy every morning. I'm the type of person who doesn't like people feeling sorry for me, so I pretended to be okay from the very beginning. What people didn't know was that I was leading a secret life, numbing out all feelings. I hid my shameful secret from everyone: my husband, my kids, and my mom. I hid from my dad, too, because I couldn't stand the thought of him watching my bad behavior. I also hid from God. That's what alcoholics and addicts do—we hide.

My world came crashing down on March 6, 2007, when my then-husband found my drugs and called the police. I was taken to County Mental Health where I was put on a seventy-two-hour hold. I've never felt so scared, confused, and alone, so very alone. I didn't know what my immediate future was going to be. It was horrifying. The third night in the hospital, I cried myself to sleep on the blue, plastic hospital mattress in a small, windowless room. What happened next is the honest-to-God truth. I remember every detail vividly.

There was a knock on the door of my room. I woke up, walked over to the door, and cracked it open to see who it was. My dad was standing there. He was wearing jeans and tennis shoes and the blue-and-burgundy sweatshirt he loved so much. He looked healthy and strong. I remember thinking how odd my face must have looked to him, a combination of utter shock and extreme joy. I reached up on my tiptoes to give him a hug, just like I always used to do. I felt the warmth coming from his body. He said, "Come with me," took my hand, and we walked down the hallway together. There was no one around. When we got to the lobby area, he said, "Look what I can do!" He jumped up through the upper floor of the building and then down through the basement and back again. He was having the best time. Then he said, "Yuh can't beat that!" and disappeared.

The next thing I knew, I was back in my room, waking up on that horrible mattress, but I was absolutely, positively sure my dad came to see me to let me know that he was with me. I was at the lowest point in my life, the loneliest I've ever been, and he needed to let me know that I wasn't alone.

I went to rehab for three months, and I've been clean and sober ever since. I've had to deal with a lot of challenges—big ones, scary ones, frustrating ones—but I know for certain that my dad is here with me brushing my hair behind my

ears or holding my hand or standing behind me. I believe my
father left this earth to better watch over the family he loves
so much. Although we'd give anything to see his face again or
hear his voice, we are comforted knowing that he's everywhere
now. His love blankets us from above.

Laura Cain

Babba Vince

My dad died when I was pregnant with my second daughter, Sarah. He had been taking care of my first daughter, Kaia, every Friday while I was at work until he grew too sick. He called her "my girl Friday." She eventually dubbed him Babba Vince when she started talking in words we could understand. He cherished his role as primary caregiver, and even if my mom was around, he made it clear that he was still in charge. As a naval officer who was away a lot during my childhood, he was really proud and excited to be a part of her life in a way that he wasn't able to be in mine.

Several months after he died, on the way to my mom's house, Kaia was talking about this and that in her cute little toddler voice, proud and strong. Her voice dropped to a barely audible whisper, and she said, "Babba Vince visits me in my dreams."

I replied in a pleasant, everyday voice, "That's great, honey." I told her that means he is done going over his lessons from life and now he can watch out for us and can go places with us that he couldn't before. This explanation satisfied her. After that, she periodically told me when he was around and gave me updates on how he was doing. She told me how Babba Vince and Sarah were getting to know each other before Sarah was born. I thought, How cool is that!

Sarah, who is now six, also gets to spend time with Babba Vince in her dreams. One time he took her to heaven to meet God, and then they went to a garden to meet Jesus. They went to a ball together and danced. One time, they went way out into space past the stars. Recently she complained about being tired and said that she couldn't get any sleep because of the adventures she and Babba Vince keep taking. I let her in on a secret about my dad: he is a champion napper. Being a former submariner, he could nap anywhere. Many of my pictures as a kid featured him asleep on the couch, wearing his navy cap. I told her, "Next time he comes, ask him to take a nap with you, and have him show you his hat."

She asked me, "What kind of hat?"

"He'll show you."

She stopped complaining about lack of sleep after that.

Over the years, we have continued to talk about Dad and how Grandma Joan misses him like we do. We keep his pictures up, and we put out yummy food just for him on All Souls Day or on his birthday. The girls will tell me if he is around, and I must say, he visits me, too. It is not the same as when he was alive but not completely different, either. Sarah sometimes gets frustrated that he died before she was born, in the way that little kids want what everyone else has. Then she goes on adventures in her dreams with him and doesn't feel left out.

Elizabeth O'Hara Yager

A Quiet Scream

I remember getting the call from my brother and sister. Dad had had a stroke and was in the hospital. Initially they thought he would be okay, and I recalled other people having had a stroke and surviving quite well. I don't remember booking the flight, but I arrived at the hospital within a day. He was awake but did not look himself. He could not talk but seemed to know who I was, or so I thought. His body was flinching awkwardly—it did not seem human, it felt strange, something was wrong. I was looking at what appeared to be my father, but innately I knew it wasn't him; he was not there. Then he closed his eyes and his brain died, and shortly afterward, so did he. I was there with his current wife, my siblings, and his friends. My mother had to wait outside; though they had known each other all their lives, the unresolved conflict between my mother and father resulted in this. The rest of us were circled around my father and watched while he took his last breath. It sounded as if his soul flew out of his body, like a quiet scream. He was not ready to go, and we were not ready to say goodbye. I was in shock. I could not believe what was happening. I could not believe that he had left the earth. It was not fair; we had not reconnected as planned.

The hospital required that we pick the funeral home so they could send his body there in the next twenty-four hours. I remember thinking that this would be an impossible task. I went to the phone booth by myself and looked up funeral homes. My crisis intervention strategies kicked in for about five minutes while I searched for a place, but at minute six, I gave up and my mother and aunt took over. Somehow I wrote my father's eulogy, and somehow I read it to a crowd of people amid the tears, shock and grief. His life had ended, and so did a part of me.

I returned home a few days later and went back to work. I stumbled a lot, could not concentrate, and felt completely alone. My stomach felt like there were a million fists inside punching at it from all directions. I could not eat or sleep. I ached for my dad and spent countless nights curled up in a fetal position crying out to him. He visited me in dreams, and I felt his presence off and on during the year following his death, but this did not replace his true presence. I wanted to touch him, to hug him, to laugh and joke with him. I wanted to tell him how much I truly loved him. Because I could do none of these things, I lit a candle for him every day for a year following his death and connected to his spirit through that medium. I also went to a spiritual healer to connect to him in the afterlife. This provided me with some solace, but it never replaced the gaping hole in my soul.

It has been eight years since my father passed away, and I still miss him. I don't feel the pain of his absence all the time, and it is not as deep, but it is there. Certain events evoke what I have lost more than others: accomplishments, life changes, marriage. Periodically, he will surprise me with a dream visit, and the impact of that visit will last for days. In a recent dream, I met up with him in a coffee shop. He was wearing the same jacket and shorts that he always wore and was sitting at a booth waiting for me. As I embraced him, a deep sob rose up from within, and I told him how much I missed him. He held me tight, letting me know that he is still around when I need him. I woke up with tears in my eyes and a deep longing for his presence. I thanked him for the visit and fell back to sleep, thinking of how he has impacted my life. I will always be Daddy's little girl, and his spirit will continue to live through me and the work that I do. I was blessed with his presence even though it was taken from me too soon. I loved my father, and he will always be missed.

Laurie Chapman

CHAPTER SEVEN:

A BLESSING IN THE SKIES

Logical thinking regarding the loss of a loved one, such as "think of it as a blessing in disguise, he doesn't have to suffer anymore," may be comforting for some, as a few of the women here have mentioned, but it did not ring true for me at the height of my grief. My grief was not rational. That he no longer had to suffer from the violent throes of cancer was certainly true; nevertheless, my dad was gone, and using the word "blessing" to describe his death, in any context, did not sit right with me, until recently.

A few weeks ago, I was talking with a friend who is known for confusing her colloquialisms, for example, she says "let's give it the world" instead of "let's give it a whirl." We were discussing a major change in her life when she said, "I really think it worked out for the best. It was a blessing *in the skies*." Her innocent blunder made me laugh, and it made me think about my own blessing in the skies: my dad.

At the time of his death, I remember having an aching feeling of wanting to know precisely where he was. Through time, I have come to understand that I won't know for certain where he is until I join him, but I have grown accustomed to thinking that he is looking down on me from up above (except when I am doing something he wouldn't approve of). I picture him amid the clouds and stars, with friends and relatives, having a jolly good time—my own personal blessing in the sky. Now, several years removed from his death, that thought gives me peace, as it does for all the women in this chapter.

Eternally Ringside

On Tuesday, September 11, 2001, my life crumbled along with the South Tower of the World Trade Center. My father worked for AON and was in a meeting on the 102nd floor that morning. "Tower two seems secure, remain where you are," echoed in the background of my father and mother's conversation. Seconds later, my dad said he saw people jumping from the high rise. My father snickered and said, "Seems? I'm going to go see what's going on. I will call you in a few, I love you." Those were the last words my mother heard him say.

That day, the world assumed that anyone who had not escaped the Twin Towers had died. I did not. I kept hoping to be the subject of a *Lifetime* made-for-TV movie in which my father would be discovered, wandering around with amnesia, in a hospital, counties away. I was in the city on September 12, handing out posters and flyers with my dad's picture and information, hoping that someone would recognize him. I went to all the local hospitals. It was so unreal to see the once angry and bitter New Yorkers come together as a whole. Everyone was hugging and helping each other instead of the typical pushing and shoving through the streets. The American Red Cross had stations set up all over to hand out food and water. People randomly asked others if they could help. It was surreal.

In the days after the attack, we received a few phone calls and misinformation, which was gut wrenching. We went from feeling overjoyed, thinking that we had found him, to finding out it wasn't him and feeling utterly dejected. We also received calls from people my dad worked with, describing the incidents of the day. One was from his boss who said that he had seen my dad and told him to leave but that my dad had said he was going back to check that everyone from his floor was out. The other call was from someone who he had worked with. He said he last saw my father with an elderly man over his shoulder on the seventy-seventh floor. The elderly man made it out within minutes of the tower collapsing; my father did not. Though my father wasn't wearing a uniform with a badge that day, hearing these accounts proves to me that he was just as much of a hero as anyone wearing a uniform. That thought has brought me a lot of comfort throughout my grief.

For up to four years after September 11th, we received multiple phone calls from the medical examiner's office, saying that they had found and identified some of my father's remains. At the time, one of my friends happened to be an NYC cop. She took my dad's toothbrush and hairbrush to the examiner's office the very next day. We received our first call when they found what they believed to be part of his rib cage. It wasn't much, but it was all we thought we would get back, so we had a small memorial service for him. Another few months later, we received a package containing one of my father's credit cards, which was slightly burned.

In 2004, we received another call and learned that the office had received three-fourths of his body—then we had a true funeral. Almost a year later, they called again to say that they found samples of his DNA on a T-shirt. Instead of having another service, we made three keepsake necklaces with his ashes in it, which will forever be among my most prized possessions.

Each time a call came, it was like rehashing the pain all over again, especially for my mother, and it meant that there was no *Lifetime* movie in my future. It was hard to take, but on the other hand, it felt like it was a way to bring my dad home. We felt like the "lucky of the unlucky" to be able to hold a true funeral with some tangible remains, considering that there were so many families that never received a thing.

Losing a parent has been truly hard. My dad was my safety net, my security. He was the one that I would go to for everything from a cut on my leg to car problems. I was Daddy's little girl and the son he never had; I was the tomboy who played with Matchbox® cars and loved sports. My father coached me in soccer and softball. When I made the varsity softball team in the eighth grade, my mother and father never missed a game. My dad would run from the train to the field every day and stay with me after practice until it was so dark we couldn't see anymore. On weekends, he would run me all around to games and practices. I have fond memories of my dad pacing back and forth on the sidelines of every game.

The field where I played little league ball and both junior high and varsity softball is right next to my father's cemetery. The town dedicated the field to my father, and it is now known as Larry Nedell Field. That token of appreciation for my father was a perfect way to honor him.

In May of 2001, I started a new sport: kickboxing. My father approved until he found out I was going to compete. I can remember my father's look of concern when I stepped into the boxing ring in front of 1,500 people. My mother said his pacing was very different and much more intense. My first fight was horrible, even though I won, so for the next three weeks, my dad helped me train. Even though he wasn't all that happy about it, he supported me one hundred percent. At my second fight, when he saw how much I had improved from the first one, he became set on helping me be the best fighter that I could. Unfortunately, three months later, terrorists had different plans for us.

It was almost two years before I was able to compete again or do much of anything. I just couldn't get myself back. At some point, I decided that my dad would not want me to stop living when someone else had made that decision for him. I went back to school and changed my major to criminal justice; it was like starting from scratch. I wanted to make a difference. I wanted to prevent any other family from having to experience what we had gone through. I also tried out for the softball team, knowing that it would make my dad proud to see me step on that mound again, and I made it. Over time, I received my bachelor's degree in criminal justice, and I got back into kickboxing full-time.

Kickboxing became my outlet. I was so angry, and I needed that outlet. Some people see a therapist; I punch bags or spar opponents. I feel that kickboxing is a way of honoring him and his memory, for fighting the way he did and for how he instilled in me a never-quit attitude. In September 2009, my trainer helped to coordinate a kickboxing benefit to honor my father and all those lost on September 11 and to raise money for a local memorial. We hope to be able to do that each year. My mother and sister aren't exactly happy with my choices of competing, but they are still my number-one fans and will be found at the ringside at every fight. In my heart, I know my dad hasn't missed one of my fights, and when I get tired or hurt he is my strength; he pushes me when I think I can't go any further. I think of what he did and how he pushed himself, not just on that fateful day but every day.

Every day of the week, he took the 4:45 a.m. train from Lindenhurst into the city and didn't get home until six or sometimes seven o'clock at night. Along with walking our three dogs the minute he got home, he was also studying at night for a certification to further his insurance career. Months prior to September 11, he received the equivalent of his doctorate in insurance—it was a series of ten tests over a ten-year period. He worked like a dog to take care of my mother, my sister, and me, and he was the most selfless man I know. He would slip me his last twenty dollars, and not have a dime to his name all week, just to be sure that I was okay. It was always everyone before himself up until his last breath.

Almost nine years later, I am thirty-one, employed by the Town of Islip, and work at Long Island Macarthur Airport in the safety and training division. I am still an active amateur full-contact kickboxer. I hold a handful of championship titles and have hopes of going professional this year. I might be the only thirty-one-year-old that is not allowed to fight without her mother and sister ringside.

My mother and sister are two of my very best friends. We had always been a close family, but my dad's death definitely made us form a solid bond. I will admit that in the beginning, it was not the prettiest of situations. How could it be? We were at a standstill for months and didn't know what to do, how to function, or how to even begin living life without my father. We took turns at who wasn't talking to whom and who blamed or hated who. It had been the four of us, and it was now three.

After September 11, we all stepped up and filled the roles that we needed from each other. My mother stepped into role of my father, and my sister, the role of my mother; the three of us became a tripod that supports and helps each other to stand tall. I don't believe the saying "God only gives you what you can handle," but I do run with the motto "What doesn't kill you, makes you stronger." The Nedell women are now forces to be reckoned with.

Though many years have passed, it feels like it was just yesterday, and I am far from over the loss of my father. I know I never will be. I miss him so much every day. Not only did September 11 take away the personal safety and security of my father, it took the safety from the world in which we live.

The images of the towers that day are burned in my mind, and constant reminders are everywhere: calls from the medical examiner, new terrorist plots being unveiled, and now the trials coming to New York City.

Though my father is not here in the physical sense, I know he is with me every day. I will never again have him ringside or have him walk me down the aisle when I get married, but I feel his presence. I try to live each day to make him proud. I daydream about waking up from this terrible nightmare. Until then, I will not mourn his death but rather live to honor his memory and make him proud of his little girl.

Jennie Nedell

Will Life Ever Be the Same?

Will life ever be as full or as joyous or as meaningful without my father? At the time of my father's death, I cried emphatically, "NO, NO, NO!" and kept that conviction for many, many months afterward. I would have bet a million dollars at that time that I would walk through the rest of my life a zombie, never experiencing happiness anywhere near the level I had when my dad was alive. The truth is that life gives us opportunities to repair the brokenness, and time gives us serenity, insight, and calm to heal the wounds brought on by such a loss. I have had incredible happiness since his death. I do experience joy, and life may have even more meaning now that he is gone.

My dad suffered for years before he died. He endured heart attacks, open-heart surgery, defibrillators, too many medications (and all of their side effects), diabetes, high blood pressure, congestive heart failure, and a massive stroke that left him unable to speak. He was a college speech and debate teacher and a master of public speaking so this seemed like a cruel joke.

Dad started having most of his health challenges around 1990, fourteen years before he died. I moved back to California from Florida in 1995, because I wanted to be near him and take care of him. I believed that my presence would help keep him alive. In the almost ten years that followed, there were numerous emergency room runs, sleepless nights listening for his breathing, thousands of decisions, millions of tears, and countless tiny cracks that formed in my heart. It was all so confusing because he still worked hard, drove his Cadillac, gardened, had a social life, and seemed very alive and healthy. Friends had a difficult time believing he was ill.

The days that Dad had no energy, when we just lay on the couch and watched TV, were difficult, but we were together. The hospital runs were horrible, but we were together. The late-night emergency room sleepovers and months of sitting in the hospital ward were misery, but we were together. It was a selfish, ego-driven desire to love being with my dad even when he was sick, but I did. Sometimes when he was ill, the moments were even more poignant, because he was soft. He was no longer attached to the anger and pride of the strong, virile, handsome father of my youth; he was simply a sensitive human being who needed me, relied on me, and loved me. He was my best friend, dance partner, and biggest fan.

When Dad died, my sister and I were away from home, teaching on the East Coast. I got the phone call, and suddenly I had no voice. I was screaming, but no sound came out. When the wailing did begin, it was followed momentarily by silence. My sister and I could feel my dad's presence; we knew he was there with us. We remained open to his presence throughout the days, weeks, and months that followed, and we experienced some moments that would be unbelievable to most people. I cherish those moments, and I am of the spiritual belief that just because we cannot see our loved ones doesn't mean they aren't by our sides, guiding us through life.

At the time of Dad's death, in July 2004, and many weeks after, I didn't think I could keep living without him. I would find myself staring at walls, the carpet, out the window. My mom said that I looked like a fragile little girl who couldn't move. I had to convince myself every day that I could keep living. I had to find reasons to keep taking steps forward instead of melting in a pool of sadness. For me, strength came from the bonds to my mom and to my sister, who encouraged me to keep fighting for a happy and fulfilling life. I also buried myself in my work as executor of his estate, as my dad, sister, and I had decided years before. I knew that if I could trudge through his very complicated estate and come out on the other side, with my sister and me in a financially sound condition, it would make my dad proud. I left my own work and dedicated a full year to his estate. It helped me get through the grieving process.

I am now four months pregnant with my first child. Of course, I wish my dad were here to see the birth and enjoy the life of his grandbaby. I will have the daunting task of explaining what a unique and incredible man Granddaddy was. I will explain how he resembled a pirate, how he looked kind of like Jon Voight, a little like Marlon Brando, a lot like Jack Nicholson in *The Witches of Eastwick*, and almost exactly like Anthony Hopkins in *The Silence of the Lambs*. I will tell how Granddaddy liked very thin slices of Swiss cheese, so thin you could almost see through them. I will tell how Granddaddy pined for the South Pacific and spoke Japanese. How he was a huge practical jokester and was in awe of beautiful fragrance, mostly from flowers. How, when people least expected it, he would "moon" them, whether it was in a crowded airport or from the top of an escalator at the mall.

I will tell my baby how Granddaddy was raised in the Chicago Syndicate but left "Da Region" and came to California in 1949 on a basketball scholarship because he wanted to get away from the corruption. I will tell him that my name, Dondi, came from my dad's name, "Don," my mom's name, "Donna," and our last initial D. My baby and his father will get to know my dad through my stories—stories that will be passed down to a new generation. My dad may not be here in his physical body, but I know that he is here every step of the way of my beautiful life.

Dondi Simone Dahlin

A Really Long Trip

My dad died when I was twenty-five. I was out of town when I got the message that he had had a massive heart attack, and I couldn't get home until the next day. I still cringe when I walk into a hotel room and see the message light blinking; that is how I got the message that he was gone.

Ah, my dad; he was everything to me, and I was his princess. I was a bit of a surprise to my parents. My sister was eleven, and my mother had been told she couldn't have any more children. My dad always called me his "little gift from God." I was loved and spoiled from day one.

My husband took the message in the hotel room the day my dad died. When he told me, it was as if time had stopped. I couldn't think, react, or even comprehend. It was my first experience with my body going into shock. I was completely numb for a few minutes, and then, the grief and awareness set in and I cried and cried and cried. My poor husband, not knowing what to do, just held me. After about an hour, he suggested that we get out of the room and go "do something." He took me to a movie, *Tommy,* based on the music of The Who. I remember being in the restroom and seeing a woman with a newborn baby. Even in the numb, sad state I was in, I remember looking at that baby and wondering if my dad's soul had been reborn somewhere that day. It was a spiritual and reassuring thought.

It has been so long since all this happened, and the details of the days, weeks, and months have faded. The funeral was more a celebration of his joy for life. Immediately following the funeral, friends of the family hosted a party. This was what my dad had always said he wanted; he was always ready for a party.

I am thankful that he was alive to give me away at my wedding, not exactly a high point in his life, because he thought I was marrying a cocky, overconfident young man. Well, he was right. For heaven's sake, we were just kids at the time, twenty-one and nineteen, but it was what I wanted, and my dad *always* let me do what I wanted. He helped us start our business, even though he thought we didn't have a chance in hell of succeeding.

I wish he had lived to see that my marriage is still intact and that the business is very successful, thanks to that cocky, overconfident young man I married. I wish he had lived to see the birth of my two sons. God, he would have had so much fun with those two little boys, the boys he wanted so much, only to be stuck with two little girls.

There are incidents in my life that I am equally glad he didn't live to see, even though I know he was there with me during it all. My experience is that while my dad is no longer here in the physical sense, he has never left me in the spiritual sense. I am not a religious person, but I am a very spiritual one. I don't consider it blasphemy that every time I say the Lord's Prayer, which starts with "Our Father," I think of my dad. After all, he is my father, and he is in heaven. My dad comes to me every now and then, right out of the blue. I can sense his presence. Sometimes, when I am sad or overwhelmed by life, I can actually feel him wrap his angel wings around me, giving me a warm and protected feeling. I know he is one of the angels, always on guard and watching over me. How I treasure this knowledge.

I believe that I will be with him when I die. I know he is waiting for me at the human version of the Rainbow Bridge. While I am in no hurry to get there, I also have no worries about death or dying. I miss him, still, but I also have him with me. He never really left me; he is just "out of town" on a really long trip. Even though I'm fifty-five, I'm still his little girl and always will be.

Jacquie Kukuk

Kissing Toads

One of my fondest memories of my dad is of his response every time I called him after breaking up with a boyfriend. I would be so upset, but he always consoled me, saying, "Just think, Lynnie, you are that much closer to finding Mr. Right!" Well, I finally did with Mike, my current husband. I had to kiss a bunch of toads before finding my Mr. Right. I am so thankful that Dad encouraged me to keep kissing until it worked.

I often tell this story to friends who have gone through breakups, and usually their faces light up, probably because mine lights up first.

I often feel that he is right here, that he can feel my emotions and hear my thoughts. It's kind of a strange feeling that he knows what I am thinking, but it's also comforting, knowing that he is still here with me. I finally understand how much people affect us in so many ways. He led by example—he instilled integrity, honesty, love, compassion, and happiness, and he gave the *best* hugs!

When we laid him to rest at the cemetery, a beautiful butterfly sat on the flowers on top of the casket. I felt that was a message from him: *I will always be with you, Lynnie.* Whenever I see a butterfly, I think of my dad. He is truly with me, forever and always.

Lynn Lee

Until We Meet Again

Dad never asked for much. He didn't care for material things. All he needed was his family, and we were the biggest and happiest part of his life. Just having us around to listen to him and spend time with him was his greatest joy.

Anyone who knew him knew that he loved to tell stories, especially of when he was in the Marines. He was sent to Korea at the tender age of eighteen and was a proud survivor. It was the most challenging time of his life—until he had five children, that is.

He was a Marine and a father but also a husband, a brother, an uncle, and a friend. He was a "do it all" guy, able to fix anything, and at times, even a "know it all." As a private man, only a lucky few called him friend, but he truly was a friend to us all. He was always there to help anyone at any time, day or night.

Many believe that our loved ones pass from this life to the next someday. We may accept death as part of life, but when it actually happens, it doesn't seem fair or real. This sadness and emptiness is so very real.

As his family and friends, we are left with to cope with his departure. We have laughed and cried together, remembering fond memories and feeling the pain and grief now that he is gone. We have depended on each other to deal with our loss because we all feel it so deeply, but we must not be sad now because he has gained the greatest gift, the gift of freedom without limitations. That is something he has not enjoyed in such very long time. He must be very happy now to be rid of those breathing tubes and oxygen tanks!

Dad was only sixty when he went to be with Him. It is

said that God takes the best of us first. He will not be here on earth to meet his future grandchildren as they are born into this world, but they will meet him someday, as we all will see him again in heaven. He is there now, waiting for us to join him, sometimes traveling around in his RV, something he always dreamed of doing. Sometimes he is riding around on his tractor, finally breathing easily, smiling and whistling. He loved to whistle! It may sound silly, but remembering this helps ease the silent pain.

We must remember that he is not really gone. His spirit lives on. He is in our hearts, waiting for us on the other side, and we will be with him again.

His last words were, "I'm okay," and we must truly believe that he is.

So Dad, this is not goodbye, but until we meet again.

Eulogy by Melinda Marie (Weiner) Lintner

EPILOGUE

Creating this book was an emotional journey for me. With each submission that arrived in my inbox, I felt a thrill of excitement at having another entry, accompanied by a knot in my stomach as I read about one more woman grappling with the loss of her father. I went through countless boxes of tissues and, more profoundly, I made countless friends. I became connected to women from all over the country who had heard about my project and who shared my passion for this mission. It was these women, and the memory of my father, that gave me the strength to persevere through long nights at my computer and the daily challenges that arise from publishing a book.

When I put the word out about this virtual meeting of the Dead Dads Club, I had no idea if anyone would attend or what we would talk about. I just knew that we had to talk. Grief is just like marriage, motherhood, and manicures: women want and *need* to talk about them, but daily life does not always provide opportunities to do so. There are few forums where we can share our stories or grapple with our grief. It is my sincere hope that my fellow sisters gain solace, strength, and inspiration from the stories shared here, that they feel a little less crazy, a little less alone, and maybe even inspired to write their own story.

As an extension of this meeting, I created a website where we can continue to connect, commiserate, and celebrate our dads. Please visit DeadDadsClub.com for more uplifting tributes, additional resources on grief, and an opportunity to share your own story.

ACKNOWLEDGEMENTS

This book would still be a mere idea nestled in the back of my mind had it not been for the encouragement and support of my husband, Steve. In the height of a difficult period in my life, he encouraged me to begin collecting stories, to start my blog, and to bring the idea of this book to fruition. I am incredibly grateful to him for his coercive urging and for his foresight as to how this project would positively impact my life.

I am deeply indebted to my dear friend, confidant, and fellow club member, Laura Lee Juliano-Henson for her insight and inspiration. I cannot count the number of emails I sent asking for her advice and guidance during the three-year process of compiling and editing these stories, to which she always replied thoughtfully and thoroughly. She helped motivate me in ways she probably doesn't even know. She also helped me with conceptualizing the book cover. It pays to have creative friends.

I am thankful for the council of bereavement experts Jan Cetti, Noreen Carrington and Katherine Sherman, all of whom provided me guidance and assistance throughout the process of editing this book. Also, a huge thank you goes to Becky Ryan and Deb Anderson, two dear friends, who were constant wellsprings of knowledge, advice and support.

My mom, Vangie Regan, and my darling daughters, Lily and Lexi, have my eternal love, admiration and gratitude for inspiring me daily to find the simple joys in life.

I am humbled and beholden to all the women who sent me

submissions, emails, and encouraging comments. Not all of the submissions I received made it into the final manuscript, but all of the women who reached out to me with stories of their fathers touched me deeply and gave me the wherewithal to complete this book. I thank them for sharing their souls and joining me on this journey.

Finally, I want to thank my dad, who taught me that I can accomplish anything I set my mind to. Here's to you, Dad.

ABOUT THE EDITOR

Mary Burt-Godwin studied sociology at the University of California, Santa Barbara. She writes for MamaMaryShow. com, DeadDadsClub.com, TodaysMama.com, and several corporate blogs, including LEGOLAND® California. She resides in southern California with her husband and two daughters. *Dead Dads Club* is her first book.

CONTRIBUTING WRITER
BIOGRAPHIES

Alisha McShane worked for four years as a teacher at the Chopra Center in Carlsbad, California, after which she founded Tranquility, a center for healing, transformation and self-mastery. The Tranquility programs tailor to individual students and incorporate Alisha's training as a Vedic master, reiki master/teacher, and registered yoga teacher with the Ayurvedic principles taught by Deepak Chopra and David Simon. Alisha works as a teacher, helping families and individuals return to their essential state of balance and peace. In addition to her work in Tranquility, Alisha helps The Soul Center in Encinitas, California, create and present programs and retreats.

Andrea Hickey graduated from the University of San Diego, earning a degree in business administration with an emphasis in marketing and a certificate in event planning. Andrea currently resides in San Diego, where she works in the event planning industry.

Amy Rueff Lepore is married with two children and currently lives in Benton, Kentucky. She has taught English in five states and two countries. She is also a freelance writer and avid reader. Every summer, she takes a group of her students to see the world. She has stepped onto four of the seven continents and is planning a trip to Australia and New Zealand in 2011 to make it five.

BethAnne Yoxsimer Paulsrud, originally from California, lives in Sweden with her husband and two sons. She teaches English at a small college and is also a translator, writer, and doctoral student. Her published works includes poetry, essays, and a bilingual children's book.

Betsy Kelleher has a degree in journalism from Iowa State University. She has written for radio and newspaper and has also written scripts for audiovisual training programs. She has published two books about horses, *Sometimes a Woman Needs a Horse: A Personal Story of Discovery of a Spiritual Message in the Horse and Rider Experience* and *MARES! (Ya Gotta Love Em): Fifty Stories to Aid and Inspire Mare Owners.* Her website is go-duseshorses.com.

Carolyn Leone is a professional costume designer for the film and television industry. She lives in Salt Lake City, Utah, with her beautiful son Jack. Carolyn is the youngest sibling of nine.

Catherine Thom studied travel and tourism before becoming a full-time autodidact, and she currently works at a law firm in an administrative position. Her writing centers on tea and books and can be found at queengata.blogspot.com. She lives with two cats in Astoria, New York.

Cheryl Barto Chandler is a wife, mom, and first-grade teacher who hails from Sacramento, California. She enjoys regaling her son and daughter with stories about Papa Tom, their guardian angel who watches over them from heaven.

Cheryl Sommese holds a BA in communication and an MA in liberal studies. She has been writing poetry since her teens but recently has begun to devote herself to the craft on a regular basis. She is a contributing poetry writer for the online magazine, *The Write Place at the Write Time.* Her work has also been published in the online venue, *Eye on Life Magazine.* Three of her short stories have been included in print anthologies through SciArt Media, and one of her poems was included in the book *Unhoused Voices: Granting Change for the Homeless* published by Sabella Press. In addition to these endeavors, Cheryl writes ghost blogs, articles, card verses, and newsletter pieces. She has volunteered for Court Appointed Special Advocates (CASA) of New Hampshire for ten years. She lives in Londonderry with her husband, Don, and her dogs, Bella and Rosie.

Dondi Simone Dahlin is an award-winning, world-renowned belly dancer. She began her career at the age of four and developed her talents over the years through national tours in Dubai, Turkey, India, Tunisia, Lebanon, Africa, Greece, Egypt, Jordan, Iceland, Spain, Africa and across Europe. She has performed for Omar Sharif on his sixtieth birthday, danced for Peter Fonda, Angie Dickinson, Dwight Yokam, and Jimmy Buffet, and danced in concert with Egyptian pop idol Amr Diab. In 2000, Dondi won the title Belly Dancer of the Universe. In 2002, she won Wiggles of the West with her portrayal of Marilyn Monroe as a belly dancer, which she continued to perform throughout Spain and Europe as a member of The Belly Dance Superstars. Today, with her sister, Titanya, Dondi teaches week-long empowerment retreats about belly dance and the five Chinese elements. See DondiBellyDance.com.

Elizabeth O'Hara Yager was born in Hawaii and raised in California. Elizabeth is the favorite (and only) daughter of Vince and Joan O'Hara. Like her father, she has held many varied jobs, her favorites being a bus driver for University of California, San Diego, a zoo keeper at the San Diego Zoo, and a theatre artist. She earned a BA in theatre from UCSD, is a Quero Apache Tlish Diyan traditional healing apprentice, and is a massage therapist and small business owner at Warm Wind Healing Arts (warmwindhealing.com). Elizabeth is married to her life partner, Dean, and has two wonderful daughters, Kaia and Sarah.

Fabiola Murphy lives with her husband, Shawn, and three children (Gage, Grant, and Stella) in San Diego in the home where she grew up with her father. She is an entrepreneur and a realtor (she represented a high-rise resort, NAOS Living, in Rosarito, Mexico). She is currently an executive recruiter and trainer for Numis Network, where she teaches others how to earn additional income while collecting gold and silver from home. She has been a part of the children's ministry at her church, Mission Valley Christian Fellowship. Fabiola's father would remember her as an actress. For ten years before her third child was born, she worked on stage as well as on TV and in many independent films.

Francine Chemnick is a graduate of the University of California, Los Angeles, where she was awarded a graduate fellowship in directing. While in Boston, where she was the artistic director of The Boston Baked Theatre, Francine directed several works and a variety of musical fairy tales for young audiences. In San Diego, she has directed for The Fritz, The Barbra Streisand Festival, and Junior Theatre, and she has worked on several productions with young actors at Hoover High School and Francis Parker School. As artistic director and a founding partner of The Muse Theatre, her productions have included original plays by local playwrights as well as renowned writers such as Federico García Lorca and Tony Kushner. At the Lyceum Space, Francine directed an acclaimed production of *Hannah and Martin*, which received a Patte Award for Best Production. In addition to producing a few short film projects, Francine is currently working on a screenplay about the evacuation of art from the Louvre during WWII.

Heather-Ann Thompson was raised in Redlands, California, and was a presidential scholar and achievement award scholar at the University of Redlands, where she graduated in 2008 with a BA in government and a minor in women's studies. She is passionate about women's rights and politics. In 2008, she was certified by the state of California as a rape crisis counselor. She is proud to have been able to work with one of her mentors, Senator Joe Biden, during the 2008 presidential race. She now resides in San Diego and attends law school.

Jacquie Kukuk loves life, enjoys being an avid Tornado Chaser, and owns an audio-video contracting business with her husband in Yuma, Arizona. She has two grown boys, two dogs, and a cat.

Jennie Nedell was born and raised in Lindenhurst, New York. She works at Long Island MacArthur Airport and competes on a high level in amateur full-contact kickboxing.

Jennifer Burt grew up in San Diego, attended San Diego State University, and graduated from Brooks Institute of Photography in Santa Barbara with a BA in photographic illustration. She worked as a photographic assistant to Ken Marcus in Hollywood and a studio manager for Dean Collins in San Diego. To combine her love for travel and photography, she became a flight attendant for Continental Airlines and has been based in Denver, Houston, and Greensboro. After twenty years with Continental, she settled in Raleigh, North Carolina, where she commutes to Newark, New Jersey, to fly the international routes, while still doing photography for family and friends.

Jennifer Kalker lives in southern California and works for The Leukemia and Lymphoma Society, work that she believes honors of her father and will help to find the cure for cancer.

Jesaka Long is a freelance writer and editor living with her partner in Denver, Colorado. She's spent the last twelve years paying the bills by crafting advertising, marketing and public relations copy; she's also a drama editor for Conclave Journal. A graduate of Colorado College, Jesaka is currently writing a memoir about her complex childhood and spending as much time as possible with her brother and his family in Texas. You can find her online at jesakalong.com.

Jody Auslund is a public relations and communications professional and aspiring model who resides in San Diego, California. She holds a BA in media and visual arts from the University of California, San Diego, and an MBA with a marketing emphasis from South University. She enjoys writing, shopping, watching movies, investing in new technologies, hanging with her Himalayan cat, Bali, staying fit, and spending quality time with friends and family.

Jo Wayles lives in beautiful Ashland, Oregon, with her husband, Alan Steed. In 1979, she gave up New England life for the West Coast and was lucky enough to find a satisfying career as a psychotherapist in private practice. She spent twenty-five years working in independent schools on both coasts, most recently as the director of counseling at the Athenian School. Outside of her family and puppy, tennis is her main passion, and it is her fondest hope to develop a decent backhand during President Obama's tenure in the White House (hopefully, that gives her eight years).

Julie Ames leads a communications consultancy, The Cambridge Group. She served for two years as the executive director of global public relations at Invitrogen Corporation, overseeing media relations, global events and sponsorships, strategic communication, reputation management, and corporate citizenship for the $5 billion company. Previously, she served as an executive in corporate communications for companies including CancerVax Corporation and BioQ. Her agency experience includes positions as vice president and member of the leadership council at the Honolulu office of Hill and

Knowlton, a worldwide public relations agency. Julie also served thirteen years with the Federal Reserve System as a policy analyst and financial services director. She is a member of several boards including the Carlsbad Chamber of Commerce, the San Diego Symphony, and the Epilepsy Foundation of San Diego. In addition to a BA in economics from the University of Virginia, she holds a master's degree in public policy from Harvard University. Julie is married to Rear Admiral Chris Ames, USN, and is the mother of two children.

Karen Vine Fuller uses the flamboyant genes she inherited from her father to make each day an adventure. She currently lives in Houston, Texas, with her CPA Prince Charming husband, Andrew, and their favorite court jester, seven-year-old Thomas. Karen's dream is to write a children's book and eventually live by the beach in San Diego, California, which she thinks is like heaven on earth.

Katey Reid is a San Diego native. After receiving her BA from Scripps College, she pursued a career in art. After a decade of selling her work to hundreds of galleries all over the world, she changed course to become a pistol-packing mountain mama. She and her family now reside on Palomar Mountain.

Laura Bozanich wrote her first full-length solo show, *Eve's Tail*, in 1999. In 2000 and 2001, she toured *Eve's Tail* to the Edinburgh Fringe Festival; it received four stars from *The Scotsman* and was called "a gem of a show!" *Monsters* is part of Laura's second solo show, *Little Eve—Finding my Voice*. Laura has also written several short plays, short stories, and monologues. As an actor, Laura has worked in theatres all over California and abroad in the United Kingdom and Australia. Her most recent credits include *U.S. Drag* (Angela) and *All in the Timing* (Betty and Dawn) with Ion Theatre, *Valhalla* (Queen), *The Killing of Sister George* (Childie), *Jeffrey* (all women), Biederman and the Firebugs (Babette), *The Ghost Sonata* (young lady), *Cinderella* (Portia), and *Annie* (Lily). She dedicates *Eve's Tail* and *Little Eve* to her beloved father, Mate Bozanich, who died of cancer when she was ten years old.

Laura Cain is a radio DJ host in southern California and spends her free time with her two precious kids, Charlie and Evan.

Laura Lee Juliano-Henson is the sixth of seven children born to her saint mother and loving father, Arthur V. Juliano, Sr. Her father always encouraged the spark in her, and she is forever grateful for this gift. You can read more about Laura Lee's life adventures on her blog wesitbyfire.com.

Laurie Chapman is a licensed marriage and family therapist and has offered therapeutic services to youth and families for fifteen years. She is currently in private practice in Coronado, California, where she provides therapy services to individuals and families. Laurie is currently a certified Eye Movement Desensitization and Reprocessing (EMDR) practitioner and has extensive training in strategic and solution-focused therapeutic interventions. She graduated from the University of California, Los Angeles with a BA in psychology and earned a master's degree in counseling at San Diego State University. She is an adjunct faculty at San Diego State University in the Marriage and Family Therapy Department where she teaches graduate students effective therapy practices. Laurie has been the associate executive director for San Diego Youth and Community Services (SDYCS) for the past eight years; she served as the agency's HIPAA privacy officer and oversaw the quality and integrity of the agency's clinical programs. She is the treasurer of the board of the Family and Youth Roundtable, a family advocacy organization. Her professional affiliations include the Council for the Human Rights of Children, the California Association for Marriage and Family Therapists, and the American Association for Marriage and Family Therapists.

Laurie Houston is a mother of two daughters and has been married to her husband, Richard, for more than thirty-four years. She is employed by the Leukemia and Lymphoma Society as a campaign manager for the Team in Training Organization.

Linda Cohen was brought up in a suburb of Boston. She received her BA from Lee College in Los Angeles and her master's degree from Brandeis University. She lives in Portland, Oregon, with her husband and two children, Gabrielle and Solomon. After her father's death in 2006, Linda began a mitzvah project in his memory. She committed to doing one thousand acts of kindness, which she chronicled on her blog 1000mitzvahs.org and in her book, *1000 Mitzvahs*, due to be published in November 2011.

Lori Landau explores the link between creativity and consciousness, while striving to spark a concerned dialogue about global issues. Both an artist and writer, yogi and mom, this native New Yorker has written for a variety of magazines including Adweek, AdAge, Elegant Bride, Sportswear International and others. She writes regularly for Technorati, and was a contributor to the Silicon Valley Mom's blog, where she wrote about contemporary issues. Her most recent photographic series titled Elemental Soul, was featured at the New York Open Center. Long inspired by Buddhist philosophy, she is certified to teach yoga and meditation. At consciousnesscreativity.com she blogs about her art, photography, and yogic philosophy.

Lynn Lee resides in San Diego, California, where she works in the event planning industry. Her passions are traveling, sailing, and helping others achieve their life goals through Feng Shui practices. She is married and has two black labs and a cat.

Marjorie Edith McCartney (Margie) hails from Pelham Manor, New York. She has always worked in the hospitality industry and currently works for PRA Destination Management as the global sales manager. She has been a tour guide in Russia, attended the 2000 Olympics in Sydney, and sung the national anthem at eight major league ballparks. She is a devoted Chicago Cubs fan and season-ticket holder at Wrigley Field and is dreaming of the day that she can walk home from the World Series.

M. H. currently resides in San Diego, California, where she works in conservation research, specializing in the genetics of endangered species.

Mary Grandy was the youngest of five children in a strong-minded family. She is happily married, the mother of one seemingly well-adjusted teenager, and working a day job in the insurance industry. She is learning to use writing as her creative outlet and therapy. She dedicates her story in this book to her dad, who understood her dreams all along.

Megan Kelleher Palmieri was born in New England to a college professor and a first grade teacher in 1975. She moved to west Texas at the age of four where she remained until college. She received her degree in English and theatre from the University of San Diego and has lived in southern California for the past sixteen years. She owns and manages a summer ice cream shop in Michigan with her husband and spends the winters visiting family and enjoying the weather and the bay in San Diego.

Melinda Lintner was born and raised in Milwaukee, Wisconsin and has four brothers. She currently lives in Carlsbad, California, with her husband, Brian, and two sons, Branden and Joshua. She has a home-based internet business called TAKE 1 that offers film industry gifts and paraphernalia (take1.com).

Mika Inouye-Winkle, Au.D., CCC-A is an educational audiologist. She earned a BA at San Diego State University and a master's degree at California State University, Long Beach. While a single mom with the support and encouragement from her parents, she completed her doctorate at the Arizona School of Health Sciences. She works in Orange County and lives in Huntington Beach with her two crazy, cute boys, Jake and Nate.

Nicole Boyle Dominguez is a marketing professional living in San Diego, California, with her loving husband, son, and two dogs.

Norma Fingert Hirsh lives in San Diego, California, with her husband, Gary. They have two daughters and a cherished granddaughter. Norma started the Child Abuse Prevention Foundation nearly three decades ago in her home and still actively serves as a volunteer on the board of directors.

Ramona (Yuhasz) Gaerin hails from Calgary, Alberta, Canada. She attended the Southern Alberta Institute of Technology and earned a degree in travel and tourism. She lost her father, John, at age four and her mother, Rhita, at age thirty-six. Ramona is a meeting planner in San Diego, where she resides with her husband, Tyler, her son, John, and their two wiener dogs.

Stacey Loscalzo is a mother, wife, friend, reader and writer. Before becoming a stay-at-home mom, she was a speech therapist and reading specialist. She now uses her love of language and literature to read and write whenever she gets the chance. As a prior contributor to the New Jersey Moms blog, her essay, "Old Fashioned Mom," was picked up for syndication in a variety of small newspapers. Her thoughts can also be found at her personal blog, lovebugandrolleypolley.blogspot.com.

Tracey Adams was born and raised in San Diego, California, at the same hospital as her father. She works in sales at an event planning firm.